More Memories of GRIMSBY

Edited by Garry Crossland, MA

The publishers would like to thank the following companies for their support in the production of this book

Associated Petroleum Terminals (Immingham) Limited

Bradleys

E A Broadburn

Albert Gait

John E Haith Limited

Novartis

A R H Tucker & Son

First published in Great Britain by West Riding Press Limited
England HX5 9AE

ISBN 1 903204 36 4

Printed and bound by The Amadeus Press Limited

Introduction

'Grim reached the shore of the Humber, right at the north end of Lindsey. There his ship lay on the sands, but Grim drew it up to the land, and there he built a little cottage for himself and his companions ... And because Grim owned that place ... all who spoke of it called it Grimsby; and so shall men call it for ever, from now to Doomsday.'

This extract is translated from a Middle English poem, written in the late 13th century, called 'Haveloc the Dane'. It tells of a man named Grim and Haveloc (also called Cuheran), an exiled Danish prince who eventually regains his fortune. Different versions of the legend give different details, but all the elements of a good fairy tale are present - a long-lost prince, a voyage across the sea to distant lands, and a beautiful princess. Also, the story offers an explanation of how Grimsby came to be founded, which finds some support in historical evidence such as the early common seal used by the town.

Whether or not the legend of Haveloc is true, it is a fact that Grimsby's haven formed a natural landing place, and it is generally agreed that the earliest settlers came from Scandinavia. They may have been Danes, on their way to attack York around 866. The early settlement probably consisted of a few reed-thatched houses, situated around the spot where Bargate, the original main route from Lincolnshire, splits into three. To one side of the settlement was a Franciscan Friary, and to the other an Augustinian Priory. The town had trade links with Scandinavia until the 14th century, but fishing was its main industry - as it was Grim's, in the legend; we are

NELC Grimsby Local Studies Library

told that he caught sturgeon, turbot, salmon, herring, mackerel, cod, halibut, plaice, skate, seal and whale.

The first Borough Charter was issued at Nottingham, signed by King John and dated 11th March 1201. Other charters followed, granting various privileges, including the right to hold an annual Fair.

Throughout medieval times, fishing remained Grimsby's principal activity. In addition, coastal trade increased. Coal was shipped down from Newcastle, and grain sent back.

Icelandic cod fishing and piracy feature in 15th century records, but neither trade appears to have brought prosperity, and the town went through a bad period. At the end of the 18th century, much-needed engineering works were carried out on the port, which was silting up, and a new dock was completed in 1800. Around this time, too, a number of successful family business were started; some, like Turners drapery business and the chemist's business that was to become R C Johnson, survived into the 20th century.

The new dock proved a turning point. Grimsby's population increased rapidly, from 1,524 in 1801 to 9,000 in 1851. The town began to enjoy better services. A Gas Company was set up in 1836, and a couple of years later gas lighting was introduced - but only lit between September and the following May. The coming of the railway gave the town another boost. The Manchester, Sheffield and Lincolnshire (MSL) Railway chose Grimsby dock as its eastern terminus, and in 1845 the dock company amalgamated with the railway company and started planning another new dock. The railway actually reached Grimsby in 1848; the East Lincolnshire line was the first to run, followed by lines to Market Rasen and then to Sheffield. Grimsby now had better links with the rest of the country than ever before. Work on the Royal dock commenced, and a momentous day in the history of the town came on 18th April, 1849, when Prince Albert laid the foundation stone. It is recorded that the stone had coins of the realm inset, from a £5 piece to a farthing, and weighed 11 tons. A statue of Prince Albert was subsequently erected in Prince Albert Gardens, and towards the end of the 1960s, before the flyover was constructed, it was transferred to the opposite side of

Cleethorpe Road in front of the Dock offices, where it stands to this day.

The Royal Dock opened in 1852, to be followed by No 1 Fish Dock in 1857, a second Fish Dock in 1878 and another commercial dock, the west arm of Alexandra Dock, in 1879. Scandinavian timber became a major commodity. A new labour force began to settle in Grimsby in the middle of the 19th century, and the Freeman Street area developed as a separate community from Top Town. In 1861 Grimsby's population reached 11,000. By 1871, 24,000 people lived in the borough, now extended to include Clee, and by 1891 this figure had rocketed to 56,000. In that year there were 10,631 houses in Grimsby. A Corn Exchange and Market had been built. More local businesses were being set up, and a number of these have found a place within the pages of this book: Tickler's jam factory, started in 1878; Stephenson's flower, fruit and vegetable business, in 1897; Maltby and Coates' bakery, in 1865; and of course the Great Grimsby Coal Salt and Tanning Company, in 1870.

Meanwhile, Cleethorpes' development as a tourist resort and residential area was accelerated by the arrival of the railway in 1863, making it suddenly accessible to more tourists. Its grand Pier, opened in 1873, symbolised its new-found status as a major seaside resort.

The 20th century saw a shift in the basis the town's economy. Some of the changes which came about are reflected in our collection of photographs. Immingham dock took on an important role. The introduction of steam trawlers brought the fishing industry to a peak, only to fall victim to disputes over quotas and fishing rights. For a time the country's docks were troubled by industrial action; the quays alongside the south arm of Alexandra Dock closed and became a retail park. Grimsby town centre was modernised to meet the demands of post-war consumerism. By the end of the century, the growth of the food processing industry had established Great Grimsby as Europe's Food Town, with a thriving economy. The year 2001 marks the 800th anniversary of the granting of Grimsby's first Charter. In these 800 years the town has come a long way - and there is much to celebrate.

NELC Grimsby Local Studies Library

Contents

NELC Grimsby Local Studies Library

Street scenes

The corner to the left of this photograph will be known to many readers as Palmer's Corner. Moving round into the Old Market Place, we come to the Globe Inn. In the days when the Corn Exchange was in business, the Globe used to be much frequented by the farmers. In 1967 it was renamed the Tivoli Tavern, and was extensively refurbished inside, reflecting a changing clientele. The outside of the premises were preserved, however, and subsequent remodelling of the Old Market Place left the Tivoli Tavern, alias the Globe, untouched. On the far corner of the block facing the Globe, on our photograph, is an outlet of Tierney's, the tobacconists. Tierney's had several shops around Grimsby town centre, and were referred to as 'under the green lamp' - perhaps some of our readers could enlighten us as to the origins of this phrase. On the far side of the Old Market Place we can see the Hovis sign outside Maltby & Coates, the long-established local firm of bakers and confectioners. The business started in 1865, and carried on until 1987 when it was no longer able to compete with the supermarkets. Many readers will remember buying cakes from there; Maltby & Coates was a traditional, high-quality firm, and in their day they won a number of awards for their goods.

The writing was already on the wall for the Corn Exchange in 1956. Part of the building had already been demolished, in 1952; and the sign advertising the Chantry Billiard Rooms did little for the dignity of the remaining part of this grand building, in the centenary year of the laying of its foundation stone on 19th November 1856. (Not that there is anything wrong with billiards, and the notice suggests that the facilities provided were equipped to a high standard.) The Corn Exchange disappeared altogether in 1960, and the space it left was turned into a car park and extension to the open air market. On the right hand side of the picture, the shops in and adjoining Exchange Buildings included

NELC Grimsby Local Studies Library

the Maypole, L & G Modes, Mossons which was an optician, Dainties, The Wine Pipe, Bowman's, which sold travel and leather goods, Stephenson's florists, R C Johnson the chemists, and along to Turners' Buildings which, after the demise of Turners, was used by the Ministry of Pensions. The Wine Pipe was a very old public house which ran right through from the Old Market Place to the Bull Ring; its premises had undergone many alterations during its 175 years or so of existence, and at the time of this picture were quite narrow and cramped. Dainties was a popular confectioners. In the early 1970s this stretch had to be cleared to make way for the new-look Old Market Place.

NELC Grimsby Local Studies Library

Above: This picture postcard provides a fascinating glimpse of the businesses which were trading at the Hainton Square end of Freeman Street in the period just after the end of WW2. On the left is R Boulton, chemist and optician. In the early 1920s, this firm was trading as Boulton & Skelton, and occupied just one shop unit. By the mid-30s, the name had been changed to R Boulton, and the shop certainly has an air of prosperity about it in our photograph, with its large, ornate clock putting Boulton's firmly on the map. Few readers will remember the name now, though some will no doubt remember the business when it was Gordon Lock's during the 1960s. Just beyond the chemist's we can see the sign for Moiser's, the very long-established suppliers of baby carriages and other indispensable items for new mothers. On the corner is an early pedestrian crossing, marked out simply by studs and yellow beacons; pedestrian crossings were introduced by transport minister Leslie Hore-Belisha in 1934, but the first zebra-stripes were not used until 1951. The van parked opposite Boulton's bears the name of F W Stevenson, who we believe was a local baker, and we guess he may be delivering to the Royal Confectionery Depot which was on this corner in the early 1950s.

Right: The high dome atop Barclays Bank Chambers was visible from quite a distance away and used to be a landmark in this part of the town; but like Top Town's most distinctive dome, that of the Corn Exchange, it disappeared from Grimsby's skyline during the second half of the 20th century. This corner of Riby Square was cleared in the late 1960s when the new road layout was introduced, and the flyover now starts around this point. Looking towards town on this photograph, we can see the old Westminster Bank, and beyond that the Post Office. Readers might also recall that the Army Recruiting Office used to be situated in this block; indeed, some will no doubt will have vivid memories of taking the King's Shilling there. National Service continued into 1960, and between the end of the second world war and the end of conscription, two and quarter million men were called up. Most young men dreaded it, went unwillingly, and counted the days until their discharge. But the only way to avoid military service was to be classed medically unfit, although in some cases it was possible to postpone for professional or academic reasons. The very last group of National Servicemen were required to join their regiments on 17 November 1960 - and everyone who had escaped heaved a sigh of relief.

GUARDIAN ASSURANCE
GUARDIAN ASSURANCE
BARCLAYS BANK LIMITED
BARCLAYS BA LIMITED
RIBY SQUARE
NO WAITING
KEEP LEFT
YJV 579

KEEP LEFT
NATIONAL PROVINCIAL BANK LIMITED
NO WAITING

NELC Grimsby Local Studies Library

the second world war they got bread from Jackson's of Hull, which was good news for their customers, as it was the whitest bread in the area. Behind the 'No Entry' sign on our photograph is R C Johnson, the chemist. This Grimsby business disappeared from the town around the turn of the 21st century, having spent some 200 years in successive premises in the Old Market Place. Mr R C Johnson took the firm over from the Cook family around the turn of the 20th century; the Cooks had taken it over from the Skeltons; and the Skelton family had taken it over from Mr Bennett, who had founded the business in 1799 when he came to Grimsby from Louth.

Left: In the days before roads became clogged with traffic, a couple of sets of traffic-lights were all that was needed to manage the junction where the east-west flow along Cleethorpe Road crossed the north-south flow down Freeman Street. As we can see, a blue police box was also sited at this spot. Cleethorpe Road runs off to the right of the photograph, and the buildings along this particular stretch had altered little in the years between 1965, when our photograph was taken, and the end of that century. However, the National Provincial Bank - one of the numerous financial institutions which used to have branches on or near this corner - turned into the National Westminster Bank, then the NatWest, then departed from these premises. The face of banking changed a good deal during that period. People used to know their bank manager personally. Loans, overdrafts, investments and other transactions were arranged in his office, often wood-panelled and smelling of pipe-smoke. As the century drew to a close, banking became increasingly automated and impersonal, with holes-in-the-wall to dispense your cash at the touch of a button, and telephone and Internet facilities to allow you to set up transactions from your own front room, day or night (unless the system happens to have gone down). With technology advancing so rapidly, the old days of banking, when people stood in awe of their bank manager, were left far behind.

Facing page, bottom: We are looking across at Turners Buildings in the 1960s, when the Old Market Place was a convenient place to park the car while you went shopping. To get from the Old Market Place to the Bull Ring, you could nip along Moody Lane. Imagine a vertical line down from the left-hand side of St James's church tower to pavement level, and that is approximately where Moody Lane was. Businesses along there included Johnson & Camps in St James's Arcade, where some of our lady readers will have bought their best lingerie - and maybe one or two brave gentlemen ventured in to buy a gift for a special occasion. Opposite Johnson & Camps was Blackburn's, the bakers and confectioners. Blackburn's was a family business, with another shop in Park Street. During

At the far end of this block in Cleethorpe Road is the Railway Hotel, where Dame Madge Kendal, wife of the famous Shakespearean actor W H Kendal, was born in 1849. A well-known actress in her own right, she frequently acted opposite her husband, and also with the immortal Henry Irving. Bernard Shaw once saw her play Rosalind in 'As You Like It'; she had a streaming cold, so the play was ingeniously adapted so that she never had to blow her nose onstage. When Madge Kendal needed to blow her nose, Rosalind fainted and was carried offstage. The Railway Hotel's main frontage was round the corner in Railway Street - which could at times have been rather noisy for the residents whose windows faced that way. This railway was the main line for the fish trains onto the Dock Estate; at busy times there was a constant stream of rail traffic, with trains up to 30 wagons long. Bedford Mill, next to the Railway, was a paper bag factory, and the two smart vans parked outside, painted in the Bedford & Gifford livery, indicate that the company was prospering nicely. However, it is other vehicle by this kerb that will attract the attention of classic car buffs. Volkswagen Beetles, with their rear-mounted, air-cooled engines and their distinctive shape, held quite a cult status during the 60s, and went on to become highly collectible in later years.

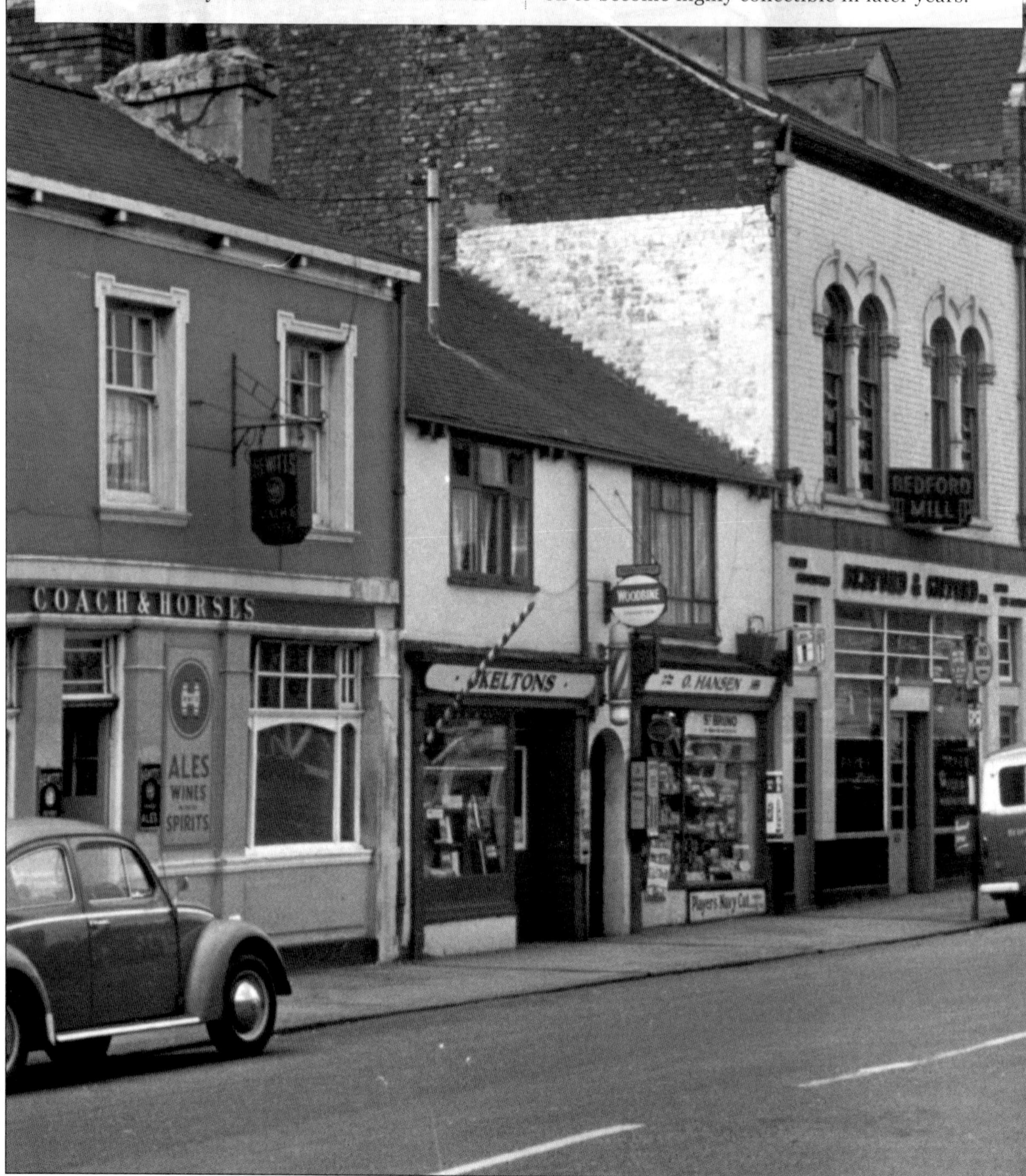

NELC Grimsby Local Studies Library

NELC Grimsby Local Studies Library

Top: Cleethorpe Road looks so deserted on this day in July 1965 that we wonder whether the photographer has crept out early in the morning to capture this view. Kettering & Leicester, the footwear shop, has its summer sale on. Rentex is promoting Supreme Drying Cabinets, reminding us of a time when the weekly wash still took up a considerable amount of time and space. By the late 20th century, most people agreed that automatic washing machines and washer/dryers were a boon, but when they were first introduced, some of us, accustomed to spending a whole morning tending to the old type of twin-tub - standing over it while it filled, sorting the clothes, taking them out of the washer and putting them into the spinner, and emptying and refilling the tub for the next load - found it difficult to get used to the idea of putting everything in together and just leaving it there. Looking along from Rentex towards the Yorkshire Bank is a sign for the Little Theatre, which as we can see really was little at that time; it was round the back of Browns' sweets and tobacco shop. Subsequently the theatre, run by the Caxtons, was able to move along and take over the large Rentex building.

Left: No collection of photographs of Grimsby in times gone by would be complete without a picture of the Black Swan Inn, otherwise known as the Mucky Duck. This well-known watering-hole disappeared in the early 1970s, so we calculate that only readers born before the mid-50s could have patronised the establishment - legally, at any rate. It was, of course, a Hewitts house. This Grimsby brewery started as a family business in 1806, became a public company in 1930, and was for a long time Lincolnshire's biggest brewery. Its main premises were in Pasture Street, on the site which subsequently became the Crown Courts, and the familiar Hewitts sign was pretty well ubiquitous on Grimsby's licensed establishments for most of the 20th century. However, the Black Swan pre-dates the Hewitt Brothers' brewery by around a century and a half. Records indicate the existence of an inn on this site since the mid 17th century or even earlier, making it Grimsby's oldest pub. By the time it finally vacated its corner location to make way for a branch of British Home Stores, the pub had stood on this spot for more than three centuries. The pleasant twin-gabled premises pictured here were constructed in the mid-1920s, and this is believed to be at least the third building to house the Black Swan.

Below: For anybody who was ever a child in Grimsby, the highlight of this photograph must be Evington's. A visit to Evington's to choose a new toy was every child's dream. When this photograph was taken, the shop had a sale on, and something in the window has clearly caught somebody's eye. At Christmas, Evington's had a Father Christmas. To find him, we are told that you used to go right through the shop, then turn left, and you finally reached a magical grotto where Father Christmas was surrounded by all kinds of exciting presents. Evington's moved to this site from earlier premises on the corner of Chantry Lane and Deansgate, and stayed until the Bull Ring redevelopment, when the business moved to Alexandra Road. However, there are other well-known names to be seen here. Stephenson's florists and the Granby Inn, a very old establishment also known as the Marquis of Granby, were also demolished as part of the town's £1,500,000 redevelopment scheme in 1971. On the right hand edge of the picture we can see Albert Gait's stationery outlet at 13 Old Market Place. Albert Gait's printing business used to have two shops in the town centre; the other one was in Freeman Street.

Right: This picturesque view of the Bull Ring dates back to around the 1940s. It would make a marvellous Christmas card. The photographer has captured the atmosphere perfectly; you can almost feel the chill in the air, and the peaceful stillness all around as the snow muffles and isolates the few sounds. The Bull Ring was the triangle between the Old Market Place and St James's Church, and at one time it was used by the town as a fish and pig market. Around the early 19th century this custom was discontinued, and the Bull Ring subsequently developed as part of the commercial area of the town, along with the Old Market Place. Stephenson's West End Provision Stores is wise to advertise Bovril in its windows - just the thing for this kind of weather! There is also a large advertisement for Palethorpes Pork Pies. Palethorpes were a sausage and pie manufacturer based in Dudley, in the Black Country; however, the name will remind local people of the well-known, high-class jewellers down Victoria Street. The Bull Ring disappeared during the second half of the 20th century when it was decided to completely reshape this part of Grimsby. A new dual carriageway was constructed so that all through traffic could be diverted away from the Top Town instead of through it. The Bull Ring, Old Market Place and much of Victoria Street were then redeveloped as a pedestrian precinct.

NELC Grimsby Local Studies Library

The Prince of Wales Theatre in Freeman Street was, in its heyday, the largest theatre in Lincolnshire. Here, posters valiantly urge people along see the famous comedian Frank E Franks in a novel song and dance show, 'The Speed Boat'. This week was their last chance to spend an evening at the Prince of Wales; our photograph was taken in the first week in June, 1936, and the theatre was due to close after entertaining the people of Grimsby for around half a century. The theatre was owned and run by Mr H J Curry, hence the inscription which we can see along the top of the facade: 'Curry's Prince of Wales Theatre'. Mr Curry also owned the Tivoli Theatre in Duncombe Street, which opened in 1905, some 20 years after the Prince of Wales. The Prince of Wales was originally built with a rather less flamboyant exterior than that seen here. However, an extensive inside-and-out refurbishment subsequently gave it this long canopy, and increased the seating capacity to 2,500 - reflecting the popularity of theatre-going as an entertainment, in the days before sophisticated film-making techniques brought talkies to the big screen and brought audiences flocking to the cinema rather than the theatre. We suspect that few tears were shed, at the time, over the closure of the Prince of Wales, as the ABC Regal cinema went up on that same spot and opened the following year.

NELC Grimsby Local Studies Library

High days and holidays

Below: This charabanc, operated by Provincial Coach Tours of Grimsby, is seen here parked in Prospect Street, Hull. We presume it has just picked up passengers who bought their tickets through Skinner's, and it seems that they are fortunate and sun is going to shine on their expedition. All the passengers are togged up in coats and hats; the charabanc does have a hood, which can be seen folded down at the back, but this would only be put up if it rained. Going along topless was all part of the fun. It's a far cry from modern air-conditioned coaches with videos, toilets and all their other mod cons and safety features ... Looking at the rather solid-looking tyres one wonders, too, how advanced the suspension was, although this was not such a problem as speeds were unlikely to exceed 20 miles per hour - just as well, otherwise some those hats would never have stayed on! Charabanc outings were very popular during the 1920s, and some firms or even well-off individuals invested in motor lorries which could be converted into charabancs. These were very ingenious, as they could be used as delivery vehicles during the week, then at the weekend you take one body off, pop another on, and hey presto! a charabanc.

NELC Grimsby Local Studies Library

Here's a picture that will bring back many memories - happy hours on the beach with buckets and spades, evenings at the Pavilion with a sweetheart, carefree days eating candyfloss or ice-cream or toffee apples or sticks of rock as you strolled along the Prom, surrounded by crowds of day-trippers and holiday-makers. This photograph was taken before World War II, and shows Cleethorpes Pier at its most impressive. The section of the Pier which can be seen beyond the Pavilion was breached during the war to prevent the enemy making use of it. This meant knocking down a considerable section in the middle, and readers may remember the inaccessible chunk of pier which was left standing out to sea. This

NELC Grimsby Local Studies Library

piece was later removed, leaving a somewhat truncated structure, 355 foot long as compared to its impressive pre-war length of 1,200 foot. The pier was first opened on August Bank Holiday 1873, making it around 50 years old when this snapshot was taken, although the Pavilion itself is more recent. A pier head concert hall was added in 1888 but destroyed by fire on 29 June 1903; a picture postcard recorded this disaster, showing smoke issuing from the hall. Three years on, in 1906, the Pavilion which we all know was constructed and became a quintessential part of the Cleethorpes experience. Near the end of the 20th century it took on a new lease of life following a facelift which transformed it into the largest nightclub for miles around.

Right: Bathed in sunlight, this photograph is a compilation of all the elements necessary for a grand day by the sea - a shop selling Wall's ice-cream, another selling Kodak film for your camera, a fish and chip restaurant, a cafe, and of course, to round the day off nicely, the Empire Theatre. Some of these features are still there - the restaurant is still a restaurant, though no longer the Criterion, and there is still a newsagents' occupying this spot on the corner of Alexandra Road and Market Street; but the Empire Theatre is sadly no longer with us. The Empire used to time its programme so that the show ended ten minutes before the last train departed from Cleethorpes to Grimsby, giving the people who had come for the day just nice time to get to the railway station and climb aboard. The parade of shops, with their very decorative rooflines, was erected in 1903 in commemoration of the coronation of Edward VII. Edward VII was in fact crowned on 9th August 1902; the date had originally been set for June 24th, but was delayed because he had appendicitis. The plaster arch visible down Market Street, by the car, had disappeared by the end of the 20th century, but apart from that the building was little altered. During the second half of the century, a mini-roundabout was constructed at this junction.

NELC Grimsby Local Studies Library

If you drive into Cleethorpes from Grimsby, this stretch of the Prom is at the far end of the seafront, down towards where the Leisure Centre now stands. Kingsway Gardens are laid out as immaculately as always, and on the left of the picture is the Lifeboat Hotel, which stood there for many a year. How grand it always seemed to us as children, with its large bay windows looking imperiously out to sea! Cleethorpes has a very long history as a tourist resort. The town was already attracting visitors by the end of the 18th century, and as transport services to the area improved, it became busier. Steam packets began bringing a steady influx of visitors in the first half of the 19th century, and the arrival of the railway in 1863 made Cleethorpes accessible to day-trippers from Yorkshire and Lancashire as well as an increased number who came for more prolonged stays. Records indicate that Cleethorpes had around 300,000 visitors in 1881. The Prom and gardens date back to 1886, and the names of many of the roads give an indication of whether they were constructed during the reign of Queen Victoria or that of Edward VII, who was king between 1901 and 1910. Queen Alexandra was, of course, Edward VII's wife. George V, after whom the stadium is named, came to the throne in 1911.

Below: Over the course of its 52 years as a cinema, the Savoy in Victoria Street also operated as the Gaumont, the Odeon - as in this photo - and the Focus. However, the builders made sure its original name and date of construction would never be forgotten for as long as the building remained standing, and even in its reincarnation as a fast-food restaurant the name Savoy and the date 1920 can be clearly seen, carved into the masonry. The Savoy, with 1,000 seats and its own orchestra, was described as Grimsby's 'biggest and best' cinema when it first opened. Many new cinemas were appearing around that time, and in fact the Savoy was one of two cinemas to open in Victoria Street that year, the other being The Globe. Cinemas were a favourite entertainment, so it was possible for numerous establishments to thrive within the town. By the mid-30s Grimsby had 11 cinemas and two theatres. Most people had their own favourite fleapit, but would happily patronise a couple of different cinemas in the same week to see different films. The post-war years saw a change in the nation's leisure habits, however; cinemas found it hard to compete with the small screen, and one by one they had to close. The Savoy, alias the Focus, gave its last showing to a pitifully small audience and closed its doors for the last time in 1977, having outlived The Globe by 17 years.

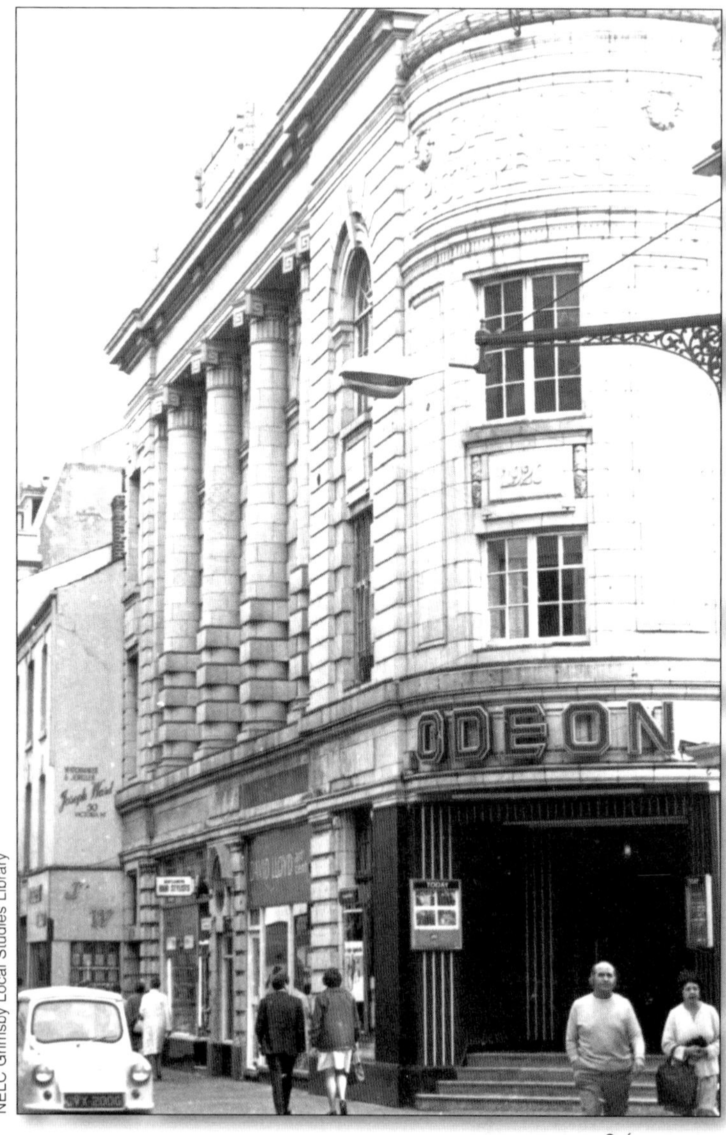

NELC Grimsby Local Studies Library

Grimsby's first special Children's Library was opened in 1940, in a house adjoining the old Victoria Street library building, which was built in 1900 and damaged by enemy bombing in 1941. In 1968 a new Central Library was built - resulting in a half-a-crown increase on the rates - and a Children's Library was opened in the basement. Generations of children have enjoyed reading and listening to stories, so what's new about the concept of the so-called literacy hour which late 20th century educationalists became excited about? The rapt attention showing on the faces of these kiddies in Grimsby's Junior Library says it all; they are on the edge of their seats waiting to hear what happens next.

What story is it today, we wonder? Alongside the children's classics that are passed down from one generation to the next, new favourites come and go, and for each generation there are whole worlds full of adventure to choose from: cowboys, pirates, secret agents, fairy princesses, giants, dinosaurs, space aliens and mischievous talking teddy bears. Perhaps the test of a really good story is if we feel that the characters are people we really know. Even if we forget the name of the girl or boy we used to sit next to at primary school, people like Winnie-the-Pooh, Alice, the Famous Five, Thomas the Tank Engine or that loveable rascal Toad out of 'The Wind in the Willows' will probably be friends for life.

NELC Grimsby Local Studies Library

NELC Grimsby Local Studies Library

Left: Many readers will have memories of day-trips to the seaside which began and ended on just such a coach as this. We thought them the height of luxury then, with their often primitive heating and ventilation systems that let you bake on a hot day and shiver on a cold one, their rather coarse upholstery that made your bare legs itch, and sometimes - if you were very lucky - a crackly radio. This one even has a clock - not digital, of course; digital clocks and watches were still unknown. As the 20th century progressed, technology affected our lives in innumerable tiny ways. How many readers remember the nightly ritual of going round the house and winding up all the clocks, in the days when most clocks still worked by clockwork and had to be wound up and put right at regular intervals? Let us return to our coach, however. We note that the driver is wearing a seatbelt - a precaution which had become second nature to every motorist by the end of the 20th century, but in fact only became compulsory by law in 1986, following intense campaigning and advertising on television and posters by the roadside. Remember the long-haired DJ Jimmy Saville hammering home the message: 'Clunk, click, every trip'?

Below: It's twenty-five past eight on a nice bright morning, and a Granville Tours coach is loading passengers at the Brighowgate Bus Station. Leeds is clearly a popular destination - are all those people really going to fit on that coach? The photograph is undated, but the length of the ladies' coats and the width of the gentlemen's trousers, as well as the style of the coach, suggests the early 1960s, in which case the journey to Leeds will not include any motorway. Britain's motorway network was to grow rapidly as that decade progressed, however. The opening of the first stretch of the M1 in November 1959 marked the beginning of a positive frenzy of motorway and bypass construction all over the country. Certainly the new motorways opened up fresh possibilities for coach operators, although at the same time the increase in car ownership would eat away at their clientele. There is no shortage of passengers for this particular trip, and a modern reader is likely to be struck by the smart appearance of everyone in the queue. No designer casualwear or jeans and trainers in those days! If you were going off for the day, no matter whether you were going to Leeds or to Cleethorpes, you polished your shoes and put on your best frock or a clean shirt and tie.

Memorable moments

NELC Grimsby Local Studies Library

A real piece of history - General Booth, founder of the Salvation Army, is seen here speaking in Hainton Square. The people of Grimsby have turned out to listen to the man who did so much to help the destitute, in the days when there were fewer places for them to turn for assistance than there are now. William Booth, born in 1829, became a Methodist preacher, and in 1865 he founded the Christian Revival Association in London. With no Welfare State to provide for those who were, for whatever reason, unable to provide for themselves, a number of charitable organisations did what they could, mainly on a local basis, run by philanthropists. The Christian Revival Association began in London as one such organisation. Renamed the Salvation Army in 1878, it went on to become an international institution. Its military-style bands - which William Booth himself was apparently rather dubious about at first - helped draw attention to the organisation, and by the end of the 20th century, everybody had heard of the Sally Army. Operating in some 80 countries, its soup kitchens and hostels for the homeless have helped millions of unfortunates; it also runs a service to investigate missing persons. Evangelism remains part of its ethos, and its officers are expected to remain teetotal.

Below right: Bringing up the rear of the Volunteer Training Corps' parade through Grimsby in 1915 is the Red Cross section - apparently running the gauntlet of a tram as the march proceeds up the tramlines. By the end of the 20th century the Red Cross had become legendary as a provider of impartial and much-needed aid to those suffering the consequences of war or natural disasters. In 1915 it was still a relatively new organisation, having been founded in the late 19th century by the Swiss Jean Denant who died in 1910. For the first year and a half of World War I, Britain's armed forces relied entirely on volunteers - encouraged by Lord Kitchener's face on posters, with the message: Your country needs YOU! However, casualties in the early years of the war were so heavy that conscription had to be introduced at the beginning of 1916 in order to maintain troop numbers. In 1918 the government raised the age limit to include men up to the age of 50, and with the men away, women all over Britain stepped in, in increasing numbers, to keep the wheels of industry turning - and surprised everybody by doing so very competently indeed.

Bottom: There's nothing like a good rousing military band marching through the streets to keep the town's spirits up - this was true during the second world war, and it applied equally during the first world war. When Britain declared war on Germany on 4th August 1914, the general mood was one of patriotic optimism. Young men flocked to volunteer for the armed forces, and many people expected us to have won the war by Christmas. Sadly, the truth turned out to be very different. By September, it was already painfully clear that the trench warfare on the Western Front was set to continue for a long time, and it was also clear that the cost in terms of human life and suffering was going to be very high. As the great British public became aware of the gravity of the situation, it was more important than ever to keep morale up. This scene, showing the Bugle Band of the Volunteer Training Corps (though there are more drums than bugles visible on our photograph) marching through Grimsby, was captured on film in 1915.

NELC Grimsby Local Studies Library

NELC Grimsby Local Studies Library

Above: These brave boys, marching down Isaacs Hill, Cleethorpes, towards the junction of Clee Road and Grimsby Road, are the 10th Lincoln C Company. In the background is the old Library, which became an old people's home. Groups of spectators have gathered to watch the Grimsby Chums' farewell march, and the poignant scene was photographed in May, 1915. Statistics of the Great War make grim reading. Around ten million people died. Many millions more were injured. The average life expectancy of a second lieutenant on the Western Front was said to be two weeks. One of the worst horrors which soldiers on the Front risked having to face was the dreaded Mustard Gas, a vicious poison gas developed by German scientists and actually manufactured in makeshift laboratories on the front line. The blinding, choking nightmare that resulted from a gas attack is described vividly by the war poet Wilfred Owen. Both sides were anxious to develop new weapons. Tanks and fighter aircraft were used for the first time, and the Royal Air Force was formed in 1918 from a combination of the Royal Flying Corps and the Royal Naval Flying Service. All in all, it was a hard-fought war, whose cruel but epic battles, such as the Somme and Gallipoli, have gone down in history. There are many tales of bravery and self-sacrifice; but the saddest fact of all is that the war to end all wars was merely a prelude to more fighting, barely a generation later.

This mountain of children was, we are informed, photographed at a Labour Party on May Day, 1923. We imagine that many of these costumes also appeared at the fancy dress parade in Grimsby's annual carnival that year; they look too good to only wear once. Eagle-eyed reader - or those equipped with magnifying glasses - will be able to pick out a wealth of fascinating details. The Daily Herald has inspired more than one competitor, and is receiving good publicity. As suggested by the outfit in the front row which exhorts us to read the Daily Herald for Labour news, for a penny a day, the Herald was a left-wing, tabloid-style newspaper. It disappeared during the latter part of the 20th century, as did another once-popular, perhaps rather more genteel newspaper, the News Chronicle. Non-political costumes include many of the ever-popular themes, and it is also interesting to realise that branded products like Brasso which we know so well were already household names by 1923. Among the longest-established brands are Horlicks, which has been around since 1890, and Heinz beans, which we have been eating since 1905. Perhaps surprisingly, we did not start the day with Kellogg's Corn Flakes until 1924, and although we think of Corn Flakes as being very British, this brand in fact came to us from the USA.

NELC Grimsby Local Studies Library

May Day celebrations have changed somewhat over the years. By the latter part of the 20th century, May Day seemed to be valued chiefly as a bank holiday, and perhaps as a chance to pile into the car and go off somewhere for the day. In the years between the wars, people were happy to stay at home and make their own entertainment. A strong community spirit existed which was to some extent lost as the 20th century progressed. National events were traditionally celebrated with street parties, with treats for all the children in the street. These parties were organised by the residents, and took place so regularly that the organisers knew exactly what to

NELC Grimsby Local Studies Library

do. Neighbours clubbed together to fund the event, the women would share out the shopping and the baking, and all the family would help with making the decorations, cutting trimmings out of coloured paper. We used to spend hours making things: if not paper decorations, then it might be fancy dress costumes like the excellent creations seen here. There is a smart sailor, and a Pierrot complete with ruff and pom-poms. There are flags, and bicycles with fancy wheels - all made by hand. Children of the 21st century might look back with pity at earlier generations, and wonder what they did to amuse themselves before computers and even television were invented; well, the answer is - they had fun!

FIRE WOOD
FOR
PASTURE St
BIKES
MOTOR BP
EXPRESS SERVICE

Among the memorable events which took place in the spring of 1923 were Grimsby's 'Biggest Ever' Carnival Parade, and the marriage of His Royal Highness the Duke of York to Lady Elizabeth Bowes-Lyon, affectionately known in more recent years as the Queen Mum. Our photograph illustrates the former event. In spite of the weather, which turned out to be nasty and cold, the Friday evening fancy dress parade was splendid: colourful, imaginative, good-humoured, and so long that it took half an hour to pass. Crowds wrapped up warm and turned out to watch and to throw coppers into the collection; all proceeds of the event went, as always, to the hospital. The fancy dress competition included categories for tradesmen, tableaux, comedy, ladies, gentlemen and juveniles. This intriguing float is pictured here in Eleanor Street. The tableau makes a splendid spectacle, although we fear that its message, while no doubt perfectly clear at the time, may well be lost on a modern reader. Another highlight of the carnival was, of course, the next day's football match at Blundell Park, billed that year as 'The Match of Surprises' between West End and the Cyclists. Tickets for the carnival cost 6d, and there were free gifts to be won - many fingers must have been kept firmly crossed in the hope of winning one of the two spanking new BSA bicycles, kindly donated by Mr Geo Hildred of Hainton Square.

NELC Grimsby Local Studies Library

Above: This ingenious float appears to be constructed entirely out of boxes of biscuits, and its message is as plain today as it was back in 1926: if you treat yourself to a Watmough's biscuit, you will be doing your bit to help a good cause at the same time! The occasion of the photograph is of course Grimsby's annual carnival, when many local businesses took the opportunity to advertise their products, help the Hospital and have a floatful of fun along the way. Watmough was already a household name in Grimsby by this time, providing employment as well as producing biscuits. The biscuit business grew out of a grocery which also supplied ships' provisions. Watmough's earliest biscuits were ships' biscuits, manufactured at the Neptune Steam Biscuit Factory in Flower Square. The rest, as they say, is history; Watmough's Biscuits became a highly popular line, and the biscuit factory subsequently moved out to Great Coates. Many women found work there, packing biscuits - a job which called for nimble fingers and good co-ordination, especially in the days before mechanisation. The smart white overalls and caps of these young temptresses suggest that hygiene at the factory was even then anticipating 21st century Health & Safety regulations - and back then, no-one dreamed of worrying whether or not foods contained genetically modified substances or animal fats. So go on, have a biscuit!

Right: In the years between the two world wars, May was traditionally the month when Grimsby turned its thoughts to the Carnival. But in 1926, people had something else on their mind. The country was in the grip of the General Strike, and virtually every walk of life was affected, from transport to newspapers - although Grimsby's Telegraph managed to keep going. The strike began on 3rd May when the Trades Union Congress called member unions out in support of the miners, many of whom had been locked out after refusing to accept a cut in pay. Many industries, including the docks, were brought to an abrupt standstill. The strike lasted for nine days, during which time volunteers stepped in to cross picket lines and get transport and other public services moving again, and the Government also took the step of calling in the Army and the Royal Navy. On Wednesday 12th May, three days before Grimsby's carnival weekend, the TUC called off the strike, though the miners' union held out - in vain - for much longer. Here we see one Grimsby firm which has made a brave effort for the camera in spite of everything. We take it that the message on the posters, 'Open the gates and let the trawlers come in', is a plea to the docks to resume business as usual.

NELC Grimsby Local Studies Library

NELC Grimsby Local Studies Library

Above: Edward, Prince of Wales, is seen here approximately half-way through his visit to Grimsby on 19th July, 1928. He had no time to get bored during the day he spent here! His first act following his arrival by car at 8.30am was the laying of a wreath on the Cenotaph, and from there he proceeded to the Fish Dock. Before coming to the high spot of his visit - the official opening of the new Corporation Bridge - the Prince had two particularly interesting and instructive visits to make: firstly to the Great Grimsby Coal Salt & Tanning Company, where he watched the net braiders at work, and then to the Grimsby Ice Company to see ice being made. The opening ceremony at the Corporation Bridge was scheduled for 11.45am, and our photograph captures the moment just after the cutting of the cord. The Prince then had the honour of raising and lowering the bridge, and he also unveiled a commemorative tablet. From there he went on to witness the paper-making process at Dixon's Paper Mill, and during the course of the afternoon he visited the Town Hall, laid the foundation stone of Armstrong Street School, listened to the singing of the children of the Children's Home in Brighowgate, and went to the People's Park to inspect Grimsby's ex-servicemen. All this and more - the Prince of Wales certainly had plenty to look back on by the time he headed back to London at around 4.30pm.

Right: A prominent police presence seems to have been deemed necessary on the occasion of the Prince of Wales' visit to Grimsby on 19th July, 1928 - or perhaps the officers of the law welcomed the opportunity to 'pull rank' and stand right at the front of the immense crowd which had turned out to see this very popular Royal personage. The Prince's visit had been carefully planned to give everybody an opportunity to see him during the eight hours he spent in the town. His itinerary took him up and down the streets of Grimsby in an open-topped car, and the newspaper offered advice on the best places to assemble in order to catch a glimpse of the man we thought of as our future king. Eager to secure a good spot, crowds began to assemble well ahead of our royal visitor's arrival, and part of the preparations included arranging for music to be provided at Corporation Bridge and other popular locations, to keep the waiting crowds amused. Flags, banners and buntings turned the town into a sea of colour: Turner's were selling small cotton Union Jacks for sixpence ha'penny (two and a half new pence), and large bunting ensigns for 6s 6d (thirty-two and a half new pence).

NELC Grimsby Local Studies Library

A sea of little faces has been gathered together for the photographer. Do these youngsters from Lord Street, Cartergate and Crescent Street realise the significance of the event they are celebrating? Certainly the grown-ups do. This is one of Grimsby's many VE Day parties, held to celebrate Germany's unconditional surrender on 7th May, 1945. In fact the war was not officially over until the Japanese surrender on 14th August finally marked the end of all hostilities. But as far as most people were concerned, once we had defeated Hitler the war was as good as won, and jubilation broke out all over Britain during May. The flags and bunting went up and

NELC Grimsby Local Studies Library

there were public thanksgiving services, street parties, Victory dances and all manner of celebrations. The sense of relief was tremendous. During the course of World War II, the Allies had dropped a reported 2,700,000 tons of bombs on Germany, and, perhaps surprisingly, official statistics showed that fewer British lives had been lost than during the first world war. But world tensions did not miraculously melt away. The Cold War lay ahead, and these youngsters would grow up amidst very real fears of Reds under the bed and nuclear war just around the corner. The sinister image of the Iron Curtain, which Churchill first spoke of in March 1946, was to remain with us for decades.

On the home front

NELC Grimsby Local Studies Library

Below left: On the home front during the second world war, the girls played their part alongside the men - although these young ladies do seem to have landed the soft option, having apparently been put in charge of opening the car door while the chaps lift the casualty up and put him inside. On a more serious note, however, women really did pull their weight and do their share of the dirty work in the war effort. They took over jobs that had formerly been the male preserve - engineering work, working on the land, bus driving, and many other physically arduous tasks - and they did them well. This new-found independence was a revelation to many women, who without the intervention of war would never have dreamt of, say, driving a bus. Having grown accustomed to what might seem a more challenging but more rewarding way of life, it sometimes proved difficult to readjust to the traditional role of housewife when their menfolk returned. Women had, literally, begun to wear the trousers. This was by no means the beginning of the fairer sex's bid for equality; the women's rights movement was well-established by this time. Mrs Pankhurst and the early suffragettes had hit the headlines early in the 20th century, and attitudes had already begun to change before the first world war. But the role of women during the second world war certainly advanced the cause of Women's Liberation a great deal in a short time.

Bottom: Two civil defence personnel appear to be practising a Fireman's lift to convey this hapless victim to safety. This photograph bears all the hallmarks of a well-ordered and peaceful exercise, rather than the chaotic aftermath of an actual air-raid - with which Grimsby became all too familiar during the second world war. Private houses, commercial premises and public buildings in the town were wrecked by enemy bombing - South Parade School was one of the casualties - and hundreds of people were injured in the raids, with around 180 lives lost. Thanks are due to the many civilians who volunteered their services in organisations such as the ARP, and spent long hours on duty or undergoing training in order to be at hand and able to help their fellow citizens when the need arose. When we look back on the war, we tend to think of it as an exciting, frightening, intensely emotional period of history, but for many of those involved it was often just plain tiring. There were so many extra things to do on top of daytime jobs, and every time the sirens sounded late in the evening or during the small hours, it meant another sleepless night for the air raid wardens and others who had to stay on duty until the all-clear sounded - and they were still expected to be at work on time in the morning.

NELC Grimsby Local Studies Library

This very well-equipped equipage has clearly been prepared with a particular purpose in mind by the Air Raid Precaution service, either in preparation for or during World War II. We are unfortunately at a loss to know what R&D stands for - surely not Research & Development? - and we hope that perhaps readers can help us out on this point. The ladders and ropes would be invaluable in mounting rescue operations which involved scaling up or down great heights, and we wonder whether this was a special unit to handle emergencies which might occur at the docks? We can, at least, explain the white stripes along the truck's rear mudguards, the rear of the

NELC Grimsby Local Studies Library

tailgate and presumably along the front bumper and mudguards as well. These were intended to help avoid collisions during blackouts. Lashings of white paint were used in an effort to make it possible for people to travel safely in the pitch black. Buses and other vehicles were given this treatment, to make them more visible to pedestrians and motorists alike. White stripes were painted around the bases of lamp-posts, road signs and other street furniture. Strategic bits of kerb, on corners and at junctions, were marked out in white. Some public buildings with steps leading up to them picked out the steps in white. White paint wasn't enough, though, and the roads claimed many casualties during blackouts.

During World War I, British troops on the front line were traumatised by Mustard Gas attacks. When war broke out again in 1939, gas attack was one of the nation's greatest fears. So millions of gas masks were manufactured, and the government arranged for every citizen to be issued with one. For babies, anti-gas attack suits were provided. Younger children got Mickey Mouse masks, which were less frightening. Demonstrations were held to show people how to use the masks, and we all knew that Hitler would send no warning so we must carry them with us at all times. House-to-house checks were carried out to make sure that every member of the household had a serviceable gas mask

and knew where it was, and some cinemas and other public buildings had a policy of refusing to admit anybody not carrying a gas mask. As the war progressed and no gas ever materialised, we became rather casual about our masks. Besides the civilian type of gas mask, there were two other types used by Civil Defence personnel: one was a heavy-duty mask connected to an oxygen supply, and the other had a rubber ear-piece so that the wearer could use the telephone. Heavy-duty masks formed part of the protective gear to be worn by decontamination squads when cleaning up after an air raid, and we believe this photograph shows the squad preparing for one such exercise.

NELC Grimsby Local Studies Library

NELC Grimsby Local Studies Library

On the move

This group of people are waiting to cross the old Corporation Bridge, which was in use from 1872 until early in 1926. Their bored faces and resigned attitudes are probably a fair summary of the general feelings towards the old swing bridge. When it was working, it did its job in that it provided a means for pedestrians and light traffic to cross, and swung aside when required to let water traffic into and out of the Alexandra Dock. However, we can see from this photograph that the bridge deck was quite narrow. In fact it was just half as broad as the new Corporation Bridge which replaced it in the 1920s. It was also extremely slow in comparison to the new bridge; the mechanism had to be cranked by hand, and it is on record that it took on average between six and seven minutes to swing the bridge from one position to the other - as compared to the one minute required to electrically raise the new bridge from the horizontal to the vertical and vice versa. No wonder some of the figures in our photograph have settled themselves down as comfortably as is humanly possible on this very plain structure, on this rather grey-looking day. They will be there for a while.

Below: With flags a-flutter and rather un-nautical crowds on the decks of the trawlers, this is clearly not just an ordinary day at the Alexandra Dock. It is the occasion of the Prince of Wales' visit. Edward, heir to King George V, had recently become Master of the Merchant Navy and Fishing Fleet, and his visit to Grimsby to declare the new Corporation Bridge officially open was one of his first opportunities to interact with the Great British fishing industry in his official capacity. The new bridge well deserved this great honour. It was designed by the engineer A G Gardner, and built by the Glasgow firm of Sir William Arrol & Co, who were also responsible for the construction of the Tay Bridge, the Forth Bridge and London's Tower Bridge. Work began on Grimsby's new electrically-operated, rolling-lift bascule bridge in April 1926. In order not to disrupt water access to the dock, the lifting section was constructed in the vertical position. This was a skilled feat of engineering calling for precise and accurate measurement, so that, when lowered, the section would be properly aligned with the rest of the structure; and it was accomplished very successfully. Grimsby was well pleased with the new lifting Corporation bridge, which was not only quicker to operate, and wider, than the old swing bridge, but which also had great aesthetic dignity.

NELC Grimsby Local Studies Library

A bustling scene on the still-new Corporation Bridge, with the building across the bridge to the right reminding us that Coal Salt was one of Grimsby's most successful businesses. It is not surprising that it was one of the companies chosen to feature on the Royal itinerary when Edward, Prince of Wales, came to Grimsby to perform the ceremonial opening of the new bridge in July 1928. The Great Grimsby Coal, Salt and Tanning Company was originally formed in the 1870s to serve the interests of the coal and salt consumers; in effect it appears to have acted rather like a co-operative, streamlining the supply chain and keeping prices down by eliminating the middleman and, consequently, his slice of the overall profit. Coal Salt took over

NELC Grimsby Local Studies Library

premises on Fish Dock Road which had formerly been occupied by another company engaged in similar activities, and as the new company grew, these premises were enlarged. When the fishing industry was revolutionised by the introduction of steam trawlers, Coal Salt was reformed so that it could continue to meet the changing needs of its customers. As a supplier of goods and as an employer, Coal Salt was an important part of life for many Grimsby folk. A 1928 advertisement for their household coal depot in Wood Street carried the proud claim that they had supplied two generations, in peace and in war. The company also carried out invaluable war work, manufacturing, among other things, various types of protective and defensive netting.

NELC Grimsby Local Studies Library

Top: This incident was recorded in Gilbey Road, probably during the late 1950s or early 60s. Gilbey Road, part of the West Marsh, used to be a main thoroughfare, and was on the tram route to Immingham. Peter Dixon's paper mill, which was honoured by a royal visit from Prince Edward in 1928, was situated at the back of Gilbey Road. The scene here shows the aftermath of a fire. The downstairs of the premises concerned seems to have been in use as hairdressing salon; it is to be hoped that nobody was under the dryer at the time! However, this location is exceptionally well equipped to summon help in emergencies, with not only a red telephone box there but also a blue police box, and the fire brigade seems to have arrived in time to save the building from serious structural damage. Grimsby's first official fire brigade, staffed by permanent, properly-trained officers, was established in 1877. Before that, fires in the town had been dealt with by a volunteer fire brigade. Readers may recall that there used to be two main fire stations: one at the side of the Town Hall, and another, constructed after the second world war, in Chelmsford Avenue. The Fire Service moved to its Peaks Lane site during the 1960s.

NELC Grimsby Local Studies Library

Above right: This view actually featured on a picture postcard of Grimsby, so clearly we were very proud of our Corporation Bus Station in Brighowgate; but it was hardly a hive of activity when the photograph was taken at ten past ten of a fine morning around the middle of the 20th century. Buses have for a long time fulfilled a dual function in the community: they take people from A to B, and they act as mobile advertisement hoardings. In the latter role, the double-decker in the background is reminding us to fill in our pools coupons ... maybe, just maybe! When the daily grind seems never-ending, Vernons and their old rivals Littlewoods have given generations of men - and women - in the street something to dream about. The Pools have been going for even longer than ERNIE; it was not until June 1957 that the Electronic Random Number Indicator, alias ERNIE, chose the winning numbers in Britain's very first £5,000 draw. By the end of the 20th century we had the National Lottery in all its various forms - roll-overs, twice-weekly draws, lucky dips, scratch cards, you pays your money and takes your choice - but many people still preferred the weekly ritual of doing the Pools.

Below: We have no date for this photograph; however, the Bedford truck places it no later than the early 1960s, while the narrow trouser-bottoms of the man standing beside the cab, in so far as they are visible beneath his overall, suggest the late 1950s. We are reminded, too, that in the days when trucks looked as macho as this one we all tended to be rather cavalier about personal safety. We rode motorbikes with the wind in our hair, we drove around without seatbelts, and we scrambled about happily on top of rather precarious loads of timber with no hard hat, no gloves, and probably no safety footwear either. During the second half of the 20th century, attitudes changed: tighter legislation was introduced, employers and Trade Unions worked out codes of practice, and on the whole we adopted a more responsible and safety-conscious culture, both in the workplace and out of it. What, we wonder, would these chaps make of the 21st century's automated, computerised warehouses, where everything is shrink-wrapped, bar-coded and checked in and out by an electronic scanner? And for that matter, what would the driver have said if somebody had presented him with a tachograph? - probably something unprintable!

NELC Grimsby Local Studies Library

The scene is unmistakable: Wellowgate crossing, waiting for a train to pass so that we can cross over and go into town. The old signal box on the left is no longer there, however, and you can no longer travel to Yorkshire pulled by the likes of the B-1 61121 which we see here, steaming merrily out of Grimsby station of a sunny afternoon in August 1965. In fact, the era of the steam engine was drawing to a close when this photograph was taken. The post-war years brought major reorganisation to the railways, following nationalisation of Britain's rail network during the war. As well as administrative restructuring, there was also the question of how the trains of the future should be powered, and this became quite a talking-point outside as well as inside the industry, with great debate amongst train-lovers on the relative advantages and disadvantages of steam, electricity and diesel. Ultimately British Railways opted for diesel, and steam enthusiasts never forgave them. It was not only the steam buffs who were sorry to see the old steam engines go, either. Legendary locomotives like the Flying Scotsman, the Mallard, the City of Truro and many more record-breaking engines had gone down in history as part of the national heritage. OK, so the smuts got into your eyes and onto your clean clothes - but steam engines had soul.

NELC Grimsby Local Studies Library

NELC Grimsby Local Studies Library

Above: Hang on, there's something missing from this picture ... The vacant site opposite, with a tipper lorry busy in the corner, is awaiting the construction of the square, very 60s office block which was due to come and squat there, providing a convenient town-centre location for a series of businesses from the mid-60s onwards. The train just about to clatter across Wellowgate crossing is a Class K3, No 61963, pulling a passenger excursion to Cleethorpes on the Sunday of August Bank Holiday weekend, 1962. Rail excursions did a great deal to put Cleethorpes on the map as a tourist resort in the first half of the 20th century. In the days before mass car ownership, most families relied on trains and coaches to take them on day trips, Bank Holiday excursions, and to and from their annual holiday. Cleethorpes was a popular destination, and during the summer months its station would be thronged every weekend with holidaymakers from Lincolnshire, Yorkshire, Lancashire, Derbyshire and further afield. Even at the time of our photograph, relatively few families had cars; statistics for the following year, 1963, showed that still only one adult in seven, nationwide, owned a car. This pattern was changing rapidly, however; ten years earlier only one adult in twenty-four had been a car owner, and in the decade between 1958 and 1968, the number of cars on the road virtually doubled.

Shopping Spree

This photograph of the Old Market Place was taken during Grimsby's trolley-bus era, but essentially the view remained the same for a very long time. By and large, shops did not come and go as rapidly then as they do now, and the businesses that rooted themselves in this area tended to stay put until they were driven out by the developers. There was R C Johnson, the chemists' business that was originally established on the other side of the Old Market Place, but had to move over when the Corn Exchange was constructed. R C Johnson stayed here until 1971, when the premises shown here were pulled down. The business then moved to Friargate, in the precinct. After a number of years it moved back into the Old Market, occupying a unit in the Exchange complex, but finally it closed down. Stephenson's, next to Johnson, was founded by Edward Stephenson towards the end of the 19th century. Mr Stephenson opened a shop to sell flowers, fruit and vegetables grown in his own gardens and greenhouses in Brighowgate. He subsequently became one of the first florists in the country to join the Interflora organisation: in the early days, the Interflora scheme was operated through a mere dozen or so florists - of whom Stephenson's was one.

NELC Grimsby Local Studies Library

Grimsby's Old Market Place featured on a good number of picture postcards, from one angle or another. This picture is reproduced from a rather nice sepia postcard, which unfortunately is undated. The Corn Exchange building was completed in February 1857, and later in that same year the market was established in the adjoining area. The new arrangement must have been just what the growing town needed: in addition to the outside market, which was originally lit by oil lamps and later by electricity, an indoor butter and poultry market was held in part of the Corn Exchange. The busy market attracted new businesses into the Old Market Place and for many decades the area continued to thrive. But change is inevitable if a town is to keep growing; there is a maxim that in business you can never stand still - if you are not moving forwards, then you are sliding backwards. In 1960 the Corn Exchange was demolished, and the following year all the facades were redecorated to create a bright, colourful new image. A decade later, however, a much more radical redevelopment scheme began, involving the demolition of the shops along the north side of the Old Market Place. The old market was closed, and on 25th March 1976 the new £1 million covered Market Hall was opened. The area was pedestrianised, with a large modern complex containing shops, offices and a pub, and the Old Market Place took on a very different character.

Below: Seen through the eyes of a modern reader, this view down Freeman Street towards Riby Square, with Barclays' dome in the distance, is very unfamiliar indeed. The pavements are packed and the road is absolutely clear of traffic. On the right we can see the Chain Libraries. Lending libraries were perhaps the 1930s equivalent of video hire shops. You could borrow books from the public library, from private libraries like this one, and from large newsagents and big stores such as Boots. On the opposite side of the street, Burton's distinctive white frontage can easily be picked out. Competition between tailors was certainly hot in the mid-1930s. Next door to Burton's in 1935 was Weaver to Wearer, trading as the Thirty Shilling Tailors; a few doors further down was a branch of the well-known Fifty Shilling Tailors chain, and near the far end, next to the Maypole, was a Thirty-five Shilling Tailors! Nearer the camera is Swann's, the pawnbrokers, which tends to be listed rather euphemistically in the street directories as 'jeweller and clothier' or 'outfitter'. However, it is no doubt true that this establishment generally did carry a good selection of men's suits: we are told that the wives of the fishermen used to put their husband's best suit into hock every time he went to sea, regular as clockwork, and go and redeem it when he was due back.

Bottom: In 1925, when this photograph was taken, the tall building on the left-hand corner was Turners, Grimsby's well-known drapers. This very old business served the people of Grimsby throughout the 19th century and well into the 20th. It is believed to have begun on a small scale around 1796. The large, impressive premises seen here must have still been quite new at the time of the photograph: the store was rebuilt and expanded after the end of the first world war. Turners Chambers were let out as offices to solicitors, insurance companies and other businesses of that nature. The drapery business closed in 1937, but the name continued to be associated with this corner of the Old Market Place. After Turners' closure, two former employees, Miss Johnson and Miss Camp, moved to Moody Lane and established their well-known lingerie business in St James's Arcade. Facing Turners is Ye Olde Whyte Hart; the olde worlde spelling on the inn sign here seems to have been a temporary quirk, although the White Hart is genuinely one of Grimsby's very old inns. It has been in existence since the 17th century, and up until the end of the 19th century the premises had stabling for up to 15 horses. In 1899 the White Hart was purchased by the Hewitt family, who carried out extensive refurbishment. In 1971, when the whole area underwent radical alteration, the White Hart was treated to another facelift.

NELC Grimsby Local Studies Library

NELC Grimsby Local Studies Library

NELC Grimsby Local Studies Library

NELC Grimsby Local Studies Library

Above: The distinctive building on the corner of Freeman Street and Duncombe Street used to be Grimsby's Hall of Science, run by Joseph Curry. It therefore seems very appropriate that the premises should have become an electrical dealers, and indeed Rayners' electrical business, pictured here in September 1965, was to remain there for the rest of the century and beyond. During that period Rayners also took over the furniture business further along Freeman Street which can be seen here trading under the name of Hardys, absorbing the premises here occupied by John Benson. On the Duncombe Street side of the building, the display windows were subsequently blocked off. The range of goods inside the shop has changed somewhat over the years. The name Ekcovision probably means little to younger readers, but those with longer memories will remember the catchy Ekco advertising jingle. Fridges, twin-tub washing machines, cookers and Hoovers were all most households aspired to in the way of domestic appliances. Microwaves and digital technology were unheard of. In the sphere of home entertainment, black-and-white televisions, long-playing records and reel-to-reel tape recorders were about as hi-tech as it got, back in 1965. But the quality of the entertainment was none the worse for that: at number one in the charts in September of that year was the Rolling Stones' all-time classic, '(I Can't Get No) Satisfaction'.

Above right: A sunny day in the 1960s seems to have inspired Grimsby's mums to turn out en masse with their infants, and Victoria Street is becoming quite congested with prams and pushchairs. The lady standing outside Woolworths, seen in profile, is wearing the stiletto-heeled shoes that caused so many headaches for those responsible for maintaining the floors of public buildings - the stilettos used to dig little round holes all over wooden or linoleum flooring. Many readers will have spent happy baby days in prams very like the one parked outside Woolworths, with the horse mobile strung across the front. The ingenious lightweight buggies which had become popular by the end of the 20th century had practical advantages, but in their own way the baby carriages of the 1950s and 60s were splendid contraptions, with superb coachwork, and robust enough to carry all your heavy shopping alongside Baby. Prams in the 30s and 40s were similar, but even deeper; they were actually designed with inbuilt storage under the padded board that Baby lay upon - you took Baby out, lifted up the board, and there you had a capacious compartment where you were supposed to keep extra blankets and bottles, but which you could equally well use for stowing your shopping.

When Mr Michael Marks and Mr Tom Spencer first opened a branch in Freeman Street in the early decades of the 20th century, their company was still trading under its original name of the Penny Bazaar. As the Penny Bazaar, the company first occupied number 104 Freeman Street, and later spread along towards Garibaldi Street, as we can see here, to take over the adjacent, more modest premises at number 106. Following the town's major facelift later in the 20th century, Marks & Sparks deserted Freeman Street in favour of the Freshney Place shopping centre. Its former main premises at number 104 remained recognisable, though altered, into the 21st century; the top of the facade, with the ornamental masonry and the Marks & Spencer name, was removed, and the adjacent building grew upwards to give numbers 106 and 104 a continuous roofline. Travelling away from the camera we find Stead & Simpson, who have a sale on. Next came Samuels - not the jeweller, but a toys and fancy goods shop; and next to that was a branch of Lipton's. Lipton's was one of Britain's very first wave of 'multiples', having been established in the 1880s, at around the same time as other famous names like Boots, Sainsbury's and the Maypole Dairy chain.

NELC Grimsby Local Studies Library

Here we are in the summer of 65, looking down Freeman Street into Riby Square. Meadow's Dairy, opposite the Freemason's Arms, may well bring back memories of all the good things they used to sell. A couple of the new shorter skirt-lengths are being modelled for us by the young ladies standing outside the Freemason's Arms. All over Britain a new generation of post-war teenagers was growing up, with more money to spend than ever before; some spent their money on cars, and most spent quite a lot on records and clothes. Parents were horrified to see their daughters going out in mini-skirts and plastic thigh-length boots, and their sons growing their hair long and wearing flowered shirts, cravats and velvet flares. Shops selling

fashionable, off-the-peg clothes for men proliferated in town centres everywhere. The menswear chain of John Collier, 'the window to watch', opened a store in Freeman Street alongside the established firms of Burton's and Weaver to Wearer. Hip chicks shopped at fashion boutiques for mini-skirts, trouser suits and hot-pants; fashionable shoe shops had strappy sling-back sandals and stiletto shoes for girls, and Chelsea boots for boys. Teenage fashion and entertainment were completely new markets, and whole business empires were built specifically to cater for teenagers. One indication of just what a serious matter fashion had become is that in 1966, the internationally-famous British designer Mary Quant received an MBE.

NELC Grimsby Local Studies Library

NELC Grimsby Local Studies Library

NELC Grimsby Local Studies Library

Left: Shoppers were out in force down the Riby Square end of Freeman Street on this day in 1962 - a Freeman Street that looked very different to the Freeman Street of the end of the 20th century. St Andrew's Parish Church lent the scene an air of grandeur and dignity. This fine stone church was built in 1870, and was constructed in the Early English style with a clerestoried nave (a clerestory is an upper row of windows) and seating for a congregation of more than a thousand. The traditional tower on the north-west side of the church was 125 feet high and housed eight church bells. No trace of the church remained following the redevelopment of this part of Freeman Street. Other businesses visible on this photograph include Chivers & Son, the butchers, and Crockatts Dyers and Cleaners which will probably be a more familiar name to most readers. The stretch beyond the church on the same side of the road once featured retail giants such as Boots, and the Great Grimsby Co-operative Store on the corner of Garibaldi Street. One landmark which did see out the 20th century was the ABC Regal cinema, which opened in December 1937 on the site of the old Prince of Wales theatre with a showing of the Fred Astaire and Ginger Rogers classic, 'Shall We Dance?'

Above: The photographer who took this picture-postcard view of Grimsby in the early 1950s had to stand in the middle of the Queen's Highway to do so - not that traffic was posing much of a threat. Today, anybody wishing to capture the equivalent view would find themselves standing in the pedestrian zone, in danger of being jostled by passing shoppers. A considerable amount of rebuilding has taken place in the intervening years, although the most striking buildings in this particular view - the cinema on the corner of East St Mary's Gate and the two financial institutions facing each other across the junction with Brewery Street - appear structurally unaltered. The parade of shops behind the photographer's right shoulder would have included such once-familiar names as Timothy Whites & Taylors, the chemists chain which later became known simply as Timothy Whites, and a branch of the Home & Colonial Stores. Younger readers may well not remember Timothy Whites, which was taken over by Boots, and are even less likely to have heard of the Home & Colonial, which was one of Britain's early chain stores. At the time of the first world war there were some 500 Home & Colonial stores up and down the country, but the name disappeared from high streets during the second half of the 20th century.

Bottom: Shopping in Top Town on a warm day in the 1960s - remember the baskets that we used to carry? Skirts appear to be creeping up above the knee, though they will go much higher than this. The 60s were the era of - among other things - the Beatles, the mini-skirt, the Austin Mini, and pedestrian precincts. With over ten million cars on Britain's roads by 1967, something had to be done to make town centres more shopper-friendly, and the solution was to divert traffic away from the centre and create traffic-free streets. One after another, towns and cities all over Britain began planning pedestrian zones. At first there was a tendency to regard these new-fangled ideas with some suspicion, perhaps considering them too expensive, too radical, and rather a nuisance. But it was not long before we began to grow enthusiastic about pedestrian precincts - not only did they offer practical advantages, but they could potentially be made very attractive, and they became quite a feature of the 1960s. The trendiest, hippest pedestrian zone of them all was of course London's Carnaby Street, which received a great deal of publicity in the newspapers and on TV. In due course Grimsby began planning a £1,500,000 scheme to redevelop the Victoria Street and the Old Market Place area - but that time had not yet arrived when this picture was taken.

Right: How odd, you might think, to see cars parked outside the Pestle and Mortar; but when this 1960s snapshot was taken, one-way traffic was permitted in the Old Market Place, and cars could be left here for 20 minutes - just long enough to sink a swift pint of Bass! This section of the north side of the Old Market Place fell outside the 1971 redevelopment scheme, but with the exception of the Pestle and Mortar the businesses seen here did not last the century out. To the left was the Fashion House, then F A Would, selling china, and then - Chambers! Remember the coffee roasting machine in Chambers' window? You could watch the beans going round and round in the barrel, with the flames underneath. And that wonderful aroma! Inside was a range of what we would now term 'delicatessen' goods, and a cafe with a trio or quartet playing for the customers. Nobody who ever went to this wonderful shop will ever forget the Chambers experience. The array of vending machines in Noble's doorway evokes a nostalgia of a different kind. Remember those big chrome cigarette machines that sold Park Drive and other popular brands? and the Wrigleys and Beech Nut chewing gum machines? You had to put two pennies in the slot for Beech Nut - then you usually had to bang the machine to get your chewing gum out.

NELC Grimsby Local Studies Library

NELC Grimsby Local Studies Library

Down at the docks
HUMBER GR

Grimsby's elegant Dock Tower is a pleasingly photogenic structure. This aerial view shows the town's famous landmark rising majestically out of the water to dominate the surrounding area; the view from the top, more than three hundred feet up in the air, is truly breathtaking. The tower marginally pre-dates the completion of the Royal Dock, having been built in the early 1850s - right at the beginning of an era of major development and industrialisation across the Humber. Its original purpose back in 1852 was to provide a supply of water at a constant pressure in order to operate the hydraulic machinery on the Dock Estate, including the lock gates, dry docks and 15 quayside cranes. By 1892, it was found that there was no need for a large tower to provide this pressure and the smaller accumulator tower, visible on the right of the lockpit, was constructed. The unique and striking design of the Dock Tower is the work of James Witham Wild and the man responsible for building it was Mr J M Rendal, who was the Engineer for the Royal Dock. We are told that more than a million bricks were used in the course of its construction, with the millionth brick being enclosed in a glass case. The Dock Tower has been designated a Grade One listed building, confirming its rightful place in our national heritage.

NELC Grimsby Local Studies Library

NELC Grimsby Local Studies Library

Above: The crew of this Royal Navy submarine seem to be relaxing and taking it easy while their vessel lies in Alexandra Dock. Grimsby was of course a submarine base during the first world war. The photograph is thought to have been taken in 1914, though the submarine's presence does not necessarily indicate that World War I had begun; submarines were frequently to be seen in the Dock in the years before the war. Britain first became interested in developing submarines around the turn of the 20th century, and the submarine was not originally conceived as a weapon of war. Perhaps surprisingly, the very first submarine had been tested a full century earlier, when an engineer named Robert Fulton built a submarine craft called the Nautilus - not to be confused with the American nuclear powered submarine of the same name which made the first voyage under the North Pole in 1958. Robert Fulton's Nautilus was trialed in French waters in 1801, but the concept was way ahead of its time, and was not developed to any extent until it became possible to use electricity for underwater propulsion. It was Germany which first turned the submarine into a fighting machine, with its first U-boat, the U1, entering service in 1906. Over the next 60 years or so the concept of the submarine was to evolve into the formidable fleet of Polaris nuclear subs which Britain had built up by the late 1960s.

Right: Here we see petroleum coke being loaded at Immingham Dock in December 1963. The coal drop being used was built on the site where, in earlier times, rail wagons would have been hauled to the top of concrete ramps to tip their loads directly into waiting vessels. The old concrete buttresses can be picked out on the photograph, and are still there at the time of writing. Immingham Dock, operational since 1911, was originally built as a coal port and was constructed by the Great Central Railway Company to handle shipments from the Yorkshire, Derbyshire and Nottinghamshire coalfields. As the 20th century progressed, additional facilities were built, including a deep water jetty to accommodate deeper draughted vessels visiting the port. By 1970 the loading of all coal had moved to Immingham Bulk Terminal, a storage and handling complex within the western boundary of the Dock Estate. Here the coal could be scooped from large stockpiles and transported by conveyor to be loaded at the adjoining jetty. The stockpiles were, in turn, replenished by coal passing through bottom door rail wagons, whilst merry-go-round trains from the coalfields of South Yorkshire and the East Midlands were drawn slowly over a large hopper. Iron ore, destined mainly for the steelworks at Scunthorpe, was also accommodated within the same terminal, which during the 60s and 70s became a very busy area of the dock.

RIMNES

ARABELLA
LIDINGÖ

Facing page: This is perhaps one of Immingham's more unusual cargoes - a troupe of circus elephants, being encouraged to take a stroll along the lock side and climb aboard the ship which will take them over the seas and far away. Chipperfield's Circus embarked at Immingham when they set off to visit South Africa in October 1964. With the exception of the elephants, the animals were loaded from No 7 Quay, and for a brief while the docks were enlivened by the unusual sound of roaring and snarling coming from the cages where the lions and tigers were awaiting embarkation. There would seem to be an element of risk in taking elephants on ships: in 1960, four years prior to the occasion pictured here, the body of a dead elephant was found in the seas off Flamborough. It was in fact caught in the nets of the Ross trawler 'Ampulla', but not surprisingly the weight of the elephant burst the net and the body drifted off out to sea again. However, we are pleased to say that to the best of our knowledge Chipperfield's Circus suffered no such mishap, and these particular Jumbos arrived at the other side safe and sound.

Below left: On this photograph we are afforded a good view of Immingham's No 1 and No 2 Quays with, in the background, 300-Foot Quay, Mineral Quay and the Tor Line Terminal. The 'Arabella', a roll-on roll-off, is seen here docked stern-on at Immingham's No 2 Quay, with a large container cargo waiting to be offloaded. The vessel next to her, moored side-on at No 1 Quay, is being unloaded by the cranes; and on the far right of the picture, running alongside the quay, we can see the railway wagons into which her cargo will be transferred. Looking across to the far side of the dock, the Tor Line Terminal is visible just to the right of the Arabella's stern. To the left of that is No 10 Quay, generally known as 300-Foot Quay, where heavy equipment passing through the Port can be handled, and to the left again is No 9, or Mineral Quay. On the extreme left, a construction crane can be seen, apparently working on the petroleum coke silos. This photograph was taken in June 1968. We understand that the Arabella was regularly used to transport Ford cars to Norway.

Left: The South Wall at Immingham Docks is seen here during the summer of 69. We have a clear view of the petroleum coke silo, and over to the right is the petroleum coal drop, via which the contents of the silo are transferred into vessels. Immingham is the only port in the UK to export this expensive 'luxury coal', which is mainly taken to the continent. The two vessels in this picture are interesting, as they serve to illustrate how the design of cargo vessels changed during the second half of the 20th century. The vessel on the left-hand side of the picture is one of the older design, with the bridge amidships. On the vessel by the coal drop, however, the bridge is to the stern. This new design was introduced during the 1960s, and made for a simpler, less fragmented layout on board ship; by putting the engine room and bridge at one end, there was more flexibility in allocating the remainder of the space.

Above: This 1961 aerial view is typical of the era when Alexandra Dock provided a nucleus for the local timber industry. Timber was the main cargo to pass through Alexandra Dock, and it was convenient for the timber merchants to store and season the wood at the dock. In more recent times it has become common practice to kiln-dry timber. However, the old practice of drying it naturally in the open air had the great advantage that without artificial heat, there was less danger of the timber warping. It was dried in Dutch barns, which were sheds consisting of two open sides and two slatted sides which allowed the air to circulate, and a roof to keep the rain off. Up until the late 70s, Alexandra Dock used to be stacked full of timber being dried or stored by numerous timber merchants. Thomson, Eyre & Denymott and Bennetts, two of Grimsby's three largest timber concerns, both operated out of Alexandra Dock. However, the requirement for companies to employ registered dock workers as part of the staff engaged in handling timber on the Dock Estate became prohibitively expensive for the timber merchants. One by one they moved away, and by the end of the 1970s Alexandra Dock had become a wasteland.

Immingham has handled a vast range of cargoes over the years. We are informed that these particular containers, being transferred to road transport in May 1960, actually contained whalemeat. The discharging operation is taking place on Nos 2 and 3 Quay. This was, of course, before the addition of No 3 Quay extension. The latter part of the 20th century saw a succession of important developments at Immingham, including the construction of the Tor Line Terminal in the mid-60s, the development of Immingham Bulk Terminal for handling coal and iron ore, and in the final decade of the century the addition of No 11 and No 12 Quays. One factor which has facilitated Immingham's continued growth was the far-sighted provision of a lock pit which has been sufficiently wide to accommodate many of the largest ocean-going vessels over the years. Its dimensions (27 metres in width, 256 metres in length, and 10 metres in depth) may well have seemed unnecessarily generous in 1911, when ships were significantly smaller that this; however, hindsight has shown the wisdom of thinking ahead and building a facility which was to continue to provide easy access to the dock for the larger vessels of the future.

regular Butter Boat service brought in Danish butter and bacon. Butter, packed in tubs, used to be stored in sheds constructed alongside the Royal Dock in 1852. Subsequently ro-ro vessels replaced the lift-on, lift-off service seen here, and in the last decade of the 20th century the Butter Boat was transferred from Grimsby to Immingham when the vessels grew too big for Grimsby to handle.

Left: This Volkswagen Polo looks rather small and lonely as it emerges from a giant roll-on, roll-off vessel onto Alexandra Dock in the 1970s. However, the lines of Volkswagens in the background are an early indication that the number of German motor cars on our roads is set to increase sharply. It is rare to see a foreign vehicle on a photograph of pre-WW2 Britain, and this remained the case for many years after the end of the war. Britain was in dire economic straits after the war, and it was our patriotic duty to Buy British, while at the same time UK manufacturers were under pressure to export as much as possible. However, by the 1970s these trade restrictions were being relaxed, and more European cars started appearing on our roads; the influx of Japanese cars was still some years away. The Volkswagen service was introduced in May 1975 on a fairly modest scale, and the import of cars from Germany subsequently expanded to become the biggest trade in Grimsby Docks. By the end of the 20th century Grimsby was handling Audi, Seat and Skoda vehicles in addition to Volkswagens, and had also become the main northern storage and distribution point for these vehicles in the UK.

Top: The drive to export as many British goods as possible was an important factor in the country's economic recovery in the aftermath of the second world war. British car manufacturers did their bit; Britain shipped out everything from Jaguars to Minis, and out of the first one million Morris Minors manufactured, 48 per cent were exported. On this photograph, taken in April 1962, the vehicle which has just left the quayside at Royal Dock is, we think, an Austin A45. Austin and Morris Motors had merged ten years earlier to form BMC, and in years to come times would become hard for the company, partly as a result of industrial action, and partly because of increased competition from abroad. However, during the 60s many popular models were produced under the Austin and Morris badges, such as the 1100 and 1300 ranges, the ubiquitous Mini - including the legendary Mini Cooper, launched in 1961 - and of course the A45. This one is destined for Scandinavia aboard the Butter Boat. The

Both pages: The decision to locate a new Tor Line Terminal at Immingham was good news for the docks, and as we can see, the opening ceremony was attended by the Mayor and other local dignitaries. The Terminal was opened on 18th March 1966 by Lady Kirby, wife of Sir Arthur Kirby who was at that time Chairman of the British Transport Docks Board (BTDB). We are very impressed by Lady Kirby's fine feathered hat. Our photographs were taken inside the Terminal's passenger building, which was in fact demolished near the end of the 20th century. In the early days of the service, the nearest railway station for Tor Line passengers who were travelling to Immingham by train was Haborough, on the main Doncaster to Grimsby line. Passengers got off the train there, and proceeded to a small building, which looked rather like a bus shelter and carried the Tor Line logo, from where they were picked up by coach and taken to the Tor Line Terminal. The Tor Line service from Immingham originally consisted of two overnight weekend sailings to and from Amsterdam per week, and one return sailing to Gothenberg. The trip to Amsterdam cost a fiver. The young lady who is pictured waving gaily at the camera is wearing a sash with the legend 'Tor Anglia'; the Tor Anglia was one of the very first pair of vessels operated on the Amsterdam route by Tor Line. The service was a success and as time went on more vessels were acquired to carry increased levels of passengers and freight between Immingham and Gothenberg; huge liners like the Tor Scandinavia became a common sight at Immingham docks during the 1970s and 80s.

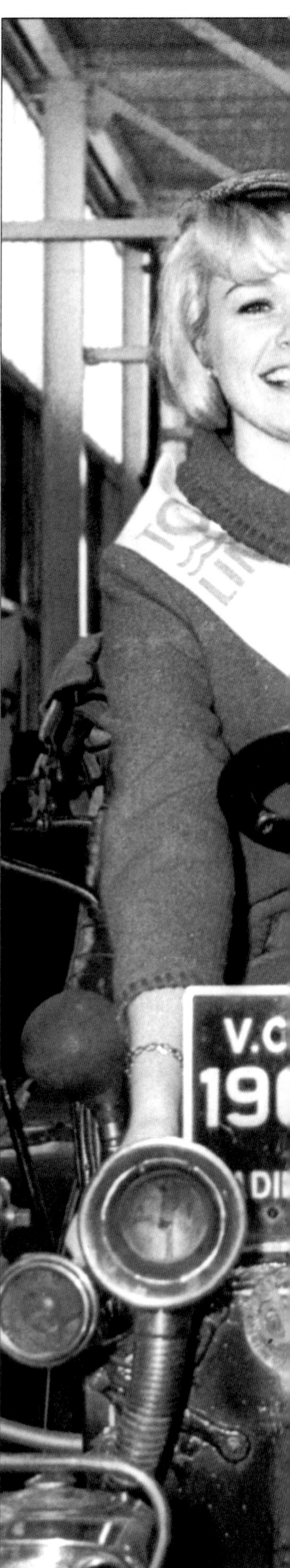

Making a living

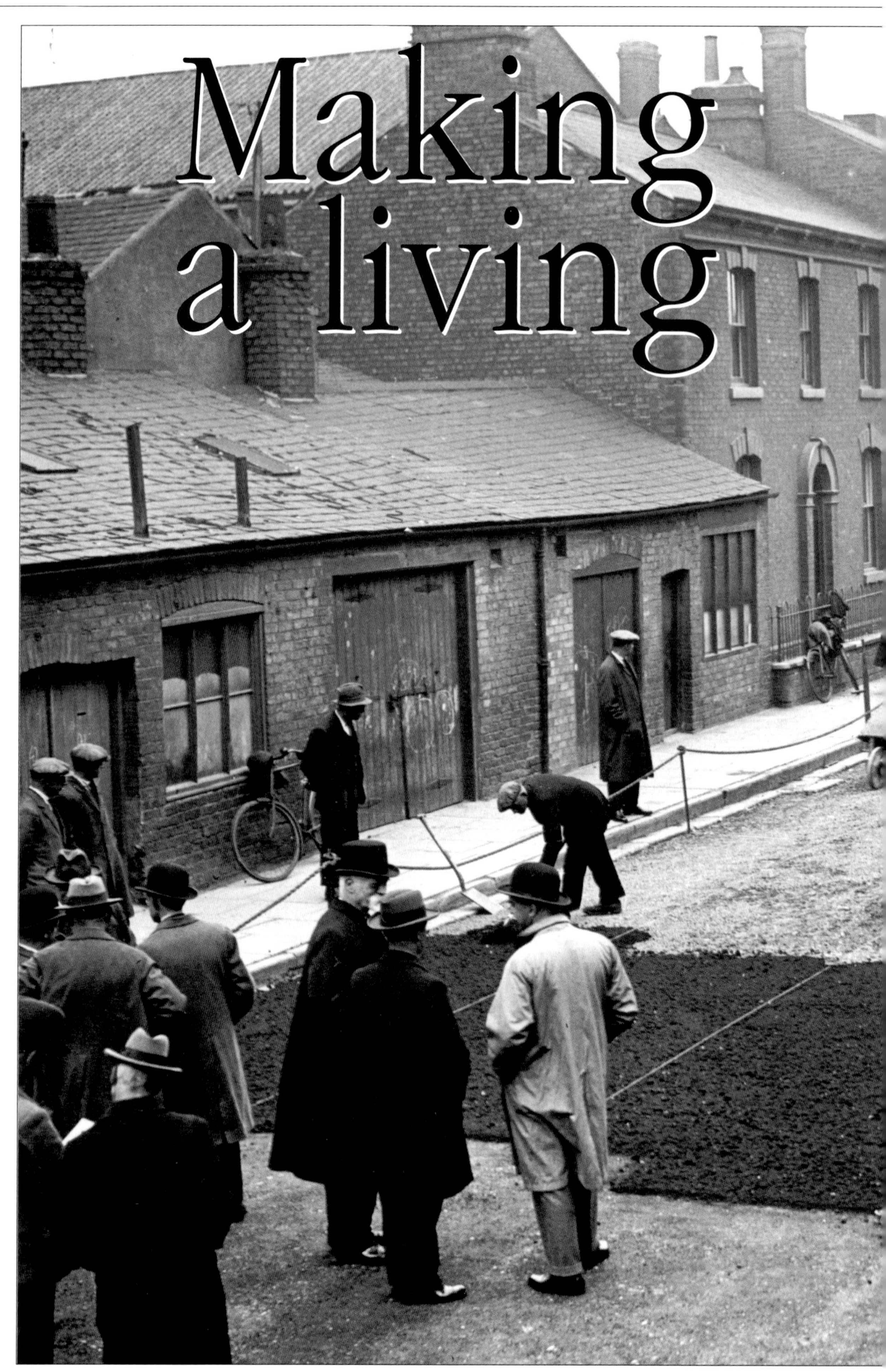

Resurfacing Queen Street wouldn't take very long these days, now that most of it has disappeared into Ellis Way; only the section nearest the camera now remains. In 1929, however, Queen Street was a little community, running from Pasture Street right down to the Malthouse, with houses, shops and businesses - including Hewitts' bottling plant, which produced the most marvellous smell. The pub on the corner was known for a time as Hewitts Tavern, but after the brewery had been pulled down it reverted to its former name, the Duke of Wellington. When it was decided to try out a new type of road surface in Queen Street, the experiment clearly interested the chaps a great deal. The road material in question was called Kyrock, and we are told that Albert Sutcliffe was Grimsby's local agent. Here we see the workmen (minus hard hats and reflective clothing - what would the Highways Agency say?) busy, May 1929 style, with handroller and wheel-barrows; a steamroller was used at a later stage in the proceedings. Road traffic was just beginning to be perceived as a problem at that time. With more and more motor vehicles on the roads, road safety became an issue and a whole new array of challenges were being created for civil engineers, vehicle designers and politicians alike.

NELC Grimsby Local Studies Library

Below right: We are told that this charming photograph was taken in 1915, when a new rag doll factory was started. Some very nice teddy bears are being lovingly sewn up by hand, and a black doll has also been made. Curiously, both these lines bring to mind the American President Theodore Roosevelt. It was because of Teddy Roosevelt that our soft bears became known as teddy bears. Cuddly bears had of course existed long before that, but they were not called teddies until a particular style of bear, called a Teddy bear, was made and distributed to promote his election campaign. The name stuck., and since then it has been applied to any and every kind of soft bear. The connection between the black-faced doll and Teddy Roosevelt is rather more sinister: soon after becoming President, Roosevelt invited a Negro to dine at the White House for the first time in American history, thereby provoking race riots. Ultimately, this new sensitivity over racial issues led to the withdrawal of many toys which had previously seemed harmless, but which were now perceived as potentially offensive. To modern eyes, some of them seem grotesque and quite unsuitable for children - there was, for instance, a craze for mechanical 'Negroes' with hideously unrealistic features - but some, like our Golliwogs in their jolly striped trousers, and this cute little doll here, were really very loveable.

Bottom: Tickler's Angels - as the predominantly female workforce of Tickler's jam factory was affectionately known - are seen here preparing and packing a consignment of Nell Gwynne Marmalade. We believe that this scene dates back to the years between the wars. The photograph originated via Grimsby Corporation's Publicity and Development Department - an indication that this company, which employed in the region of 1,500 workers, held a position of some importance in the town's economy. The firm of T G Tickler Limited was founded in 1878, and in the early days its weekly output totalled around one ton. Half a century later the company was producing 120 tons of marmalade a day, and had factories at Grimsby and Southwell. During the first world war Tickler's were responsible for shipping jam out to the soldiers on the Western Front, and, with supplies severely disrupted, they had to exercise considerable ingenuity in concocting jam out of whatever ingredients they could get their hands on. Reminiscences from that era sometimes mention the rather unusual flavours that turned up. The company's founder Mr T G Tickler was a prominent local figure, and during the first world war he was MP for the Borough, a position which he held from 1914 to 1922.

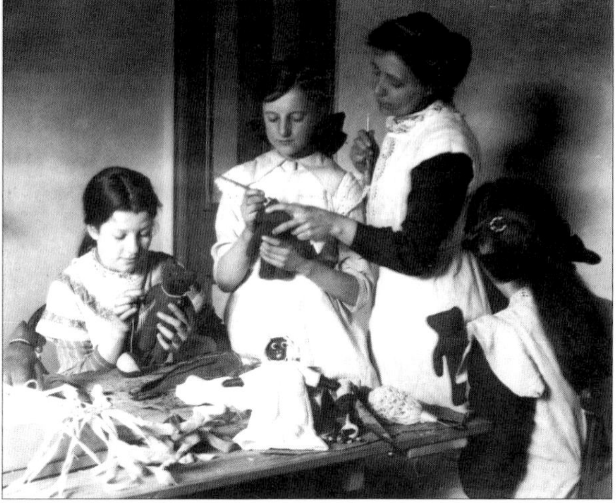

NELC Grimsby Local Studies Library

NELC Grimsby Local Studies Library

NELC Grimsby Local Studies Library

Traditionally, the fishing industry has always provided employment for many people besides the trawlermen themselves. There were jobs to be had on the docks, both dryside and wetside. There were various opportunities in the fish processing factories. And, as we see here, a constant supply of nets was needed. Netmaking and repairing was women's work, and like many other tasks it required nimble fingers. Compared to some of the other jobs that women did, working conditions were good - no wonder these lasses are smiling! They are indoors, protected from the weather, and they can even sit down if they wish. It is also much kinder to the hands than, say, salting cod, back in the days when salt was the only preservative. Salt opened every cut and graze on your hands, and stung terribly; so the girls used to wrap bandages round their fingers as a precaution before handling the salt. These net braiders are believed to be employed by the Great Grimsby Coal Salt & Tanning Company, probably in the inter-war years, and that being the case, the nets might be destined either for local trawlers or for export; the company exported quantities of nets and gear to other parts of the world. Some women braided nets at home, and got paid per panel of net. Youngsters would often do a few panels, to earn themselves a few coppers.

NELC Grimsby Local Studies Library

Left: Grimsby's two main parks, People's Park and Grant Thorold Park, were given to the town by its two main landowners, Edward Heneage - who later became Lord Heneage - and Alexandre William Grant Thorold. Whilst both men owned large areas of land within the Borough, they were unable to gain direct access to the docks. However, Lord Heneage eventually formed an arrangement with the Freemen of the town who granted him permission to link his streets into Freeman Street. This incensed Grant Thorold who approached Lord Heneage for a right of way over his land in order to gain similar privileges. Lord Heneage refused on the grounds of potential commercial suicide, but after 20 years of negotiation he finally relented - on the understanding that Grant Thorold was to donate an area of his estate for a park in the same way as Lord Heneage had created People's Park. A nine-acre site bounded by Durban Road, Robert Street, Stanley Street and Humberstone Road was opened on 30th June 1904. An inscribed plaque tells us that the opening ceremony was performed by William Codey, alias Buffalo Bill. It is true that People's Park has a lake and Grant Thorold doesn't; but what could be more pleasing than the hazy, romantic scene pictured here at dusk, with the shadows lengthening and a silhouetted figure serenely sweeping leaves as the sun goes down on a perfect autumn day.

Above: In 1965 Grimsby Corporation had a splendid new power station built on Moss Road. This photograph shows the view from the front. Around the back were two huge cooling towers; we can just catch a glimpse of them behind the chimneys above the roofline, in approximately the middle of the building. Where power was concerned, we went through a sharp learning curve during the 20th century. Electricity was still a new and exciting phenomenon in the early years of that century. When Edison's electric lighting system was first installed in houses, people thought it was the next thing to magic. In the early days, there was no National Grid, and towns generated their own electricity supply at whatever voltage they thought best. By the second half of the century, electricity had become an essential part of everyday life, with many advantages both for industry and for the domestic consumer. The problems of relying on coal to heat our homes had already been discovered - it filled the air with soot and helped create smog. With more sophisticated methods of heating our houses available, the Clean Air Act was passed in 1956, and we thought the energy problem was solved ... and then, just when we all took for granted our right to unlimited power supplies at the touch of a button, scientists discovered the greenhouse effect and environmentalists showed us that we were using up the earth's resources ...

Cementing a fine tradition

Freshney Place shopping centre, Grimsby is a familiar sight to many readers but how many know that a local company gained the contract to carry out all the floor screeding, the ceramic wall tiling, the ceramic floor tiling to all the malls and all the plastering, to what was the largest single building project the town had seen. The company in question is ARH Tucker & Sons (Cleethorpes) Ltd, which is based in Imperial Avenue, Cleethorpes. The company was established in 1930 by Arthur Roland Henry Tucker (known universally as ARH), who set up in business once he had completed his apprenticeship as a plasterer.

ARH began taking on plastering contracts and operated his business from his home in Blundell Avenue, Cleethorpes. He was the eldest of a family of six boys and two girls. No less than four of his brothers worked for him at one time- their other brother Eric owned the donkeys which gave so much pleasure to so many children on Cleethorpes beach. Of the four who worked for ARH, George, Harry and Horace all moved on to start businesses of their own, but Leslie stayed with ARH until his own retirement in 1994.

In 1933 ARH moved with his family to 18 Imperial Avenue, later acquiring and moving into number five. These were both ARH's homes as well as his offices, but since 1965 number five has been exclusively used as an office and still serves as a base for the company.

On the declaration of war in 1939, ARH undertook work for the Ministry of Defence building Anderson shelters but was called up in 1942 to serve with the Royal Engineers. At the end of the war in 1945, ARH returned home to resume his activities once more, this being made possible by his registration as a contractor by the Ministry of Works, a necessary requirement for any one wanting to run their own businesses immediately after the war. The company soon began to grow and in 1947 ARH was joined by his eldest son Roland who was indentured to him as an apprentice plasterer, being followed the next year by his middle son Arthur, also indentured as an apprentice plasterer. The company became a limited one in 1950, and ARH made both his sons directors in the late 1950s.

In 1964 Roland left to start out on his own leaving the two generations of Arthurs in the business, ARH who did all the estimating and Arthur who became Contracts Manager. It was during this time that the company started to diversify into floor screeding and ceramic wall and floor tiling. This became necessary as by the late 1960s the building industrys demand for the traditional skills of wet plastering had started to decline as new methods and types of construction began to take over.

The 1970s heralded even more changes within the construction industry and there was an almost universal move away from employment towards self-employment, but Tuckers preferred to continue the tradition of employing and training apprentices, a system which has served the trade and the people concerned very well over

Below: *One of company's vehicles outside the new cold store being built for Salvesens in Grimsby. The largest in Europe at the time.*

the years. Many of the apprentices such as Terry Fay who joined in 1955, Colin Ayres, 1959 and Terry Wishart, 1962 are still with the company, having stayed with it throughout their working lives.

During the expansion of the 1960s, Arthur Snell joined the company as a surveyor and Marilyn Tucker joined her husband to help cope with the increase in workload. In 1985 Arthur was made a director of the company and has now completed over 36 years of service.

As the 1970s progressed Arthur Tucker decided it was once again time to broaden the company's skills base and dry wall construction - metal stud partitioning was added, as well as the formation of a new company to build houses. 1979 saw John, Arthur's son, the third generation of the family to join the company as a qualified quantity surveyor. This enabled Arthur to concentrate more upon the house building side and to further develop new business. This culminated in a third company being formed, A Tucker (Flooring Services) Ltd, to undertake vinyl flooring, contract carpeting and the like, to compliment the range of floor finishes already undertaken by the plastering company. This saw John's wife Susan, join the company on the administration side alongside the existing staff with a further addition, from college, in 1986 of Donna Barrs who is just about to complete fifteen years with the company.

1980 saw the fruition of Arthur's business skills and hard work with many large and unusual contracts being undertaken, one of which is pictured above. This was the floating hotel built to accommodate the troops sent out to the Falkland Islands after its recapture from the Argentinians, until more permanent accommodation could be built on dry land. Over fourteen thousand square metres of vinyl flooring and screeding being laid in this one contract alone.

In 1992 Arthur followed his father into retirement from both the plastering and flooring companies, but he continued to run his building company until his early and untimely death in 1995. This caused a radical rethink into the structure of the companies and it was decided that to enable John to concentrate on the core business of plastering, the flooring company should be sold to its manager, this happening in 1999. The start of the new millennium has seen the company still occupying its prominent place within the local building industry and it is hoped this will continue up to and past its centenary year in 2030.

Above: *The floating hotel constructed for the army after the recapture of the Falkland Islands.*
Below: *Leslie Tucker, Arthur Tucker, Bob McKenna and Jack Hollinshead receiving gold watches from ARH and ACE Tucker after 25 years service in 1972.*

Fuelling the nation

Oil. Where would we be without it? The whole world economy runs on petroleum based products and over the course of the last 100 years ever more sophisticated means for their distribution have been utilised.

Associated Petroleum Terminals (Immingham) Limited, known as APT, may not be one of the most high profile companies you are aware of but its operation and development has been vital both locally and nationally. It handles the various vessels and co-ordinates the loading and discharging of oil in its various forms by the two local refineries. These two refineries, Lindsey Oil Refinery (owned by Total Fina Elf) and Conoco, jointly own APT which operates three marine terminals on the south bank of the River Humber: Immingham Oil Terminal (IOT), South Killingholme Jetty (SKJ) and the Immingham Gas Terminal (IGT).

APT started life in February 1969 with just 23 employees, 18 of them working shifts. Operations commenced in April 1969 when MV Alexandre I discharged 31,000 tonnes of Algerian crude to Lindsey Oil Refinery via Main Berth No. 2.

From the outset there was a lot of small barge and river traffic loaded over the Finger Pier at IOT and it was not unusual in the early 1970s to see up to 25 barges a day loading for various inland docks and wharves - although today five vessels counts as a busy day for barge operations.

Barge sizes, however, were smaller in those early days, with anything between 100 to 250 tonnes regarded at the time as big. Today barges range up to 1,000 tonnes.

Back in the 1970s much of the oil was shipped by barge to both Grimsby and Hull Fish Docks to bunker the deep sea fishing fleet, which today has sadly all but gone. Cargoes were also sent on the inland waterways up the Trent to various wharves and power stations and on past Newark. Cargoes also went up the Ouse to York and beyond into the inland waterway at Goole and Keedby to Leeds, Knottingley and surrounding areas.

Coasters of up to 6,000 tonnes were also loaded at the Finger Pier, taking cargoes to ports around the British Isles and nearby continent.

Initially the two available main berths at the end of the jetty in the deep water were predominently used to import crude oil from the Middle East and North Africa - North Sea crude did not come ashore at APT until 1971. The ships got bigger throughout the 1970s: the first 50,000, 100,000 and 200,000 tonne ships to enter the Humber each in turn making headlines in the Grimsby Evening Telegraph. The biggest vessel to use APT would eventually be the double hulled Golar Edinburgh in May 1996, weighing in at 302,000 tonnes carrying capacity. This equates to a total full cargo of 355,300,000 ltrs.

In June 1994 the largest expansion to Immingham Oil Terminal was completed when the new Berth 3 was commissioned, significantly reducing the time the large vessels had to wait for a vacant berth and giving more capacity.

APT operations at the South Killingholme Jetty commenced on 6th June 1981 with the export of 1,200 tonnes of propane from Lindsey Oil Refinery on MV Hestia. The jetty operation was formally taken over by APT in January 1982.

Above: *A view of Immingham Oil Terminal in the mid 1980s, showing one of the main deep-water berths at the forefront, 1,000 yards into the river and two coasters on the Finger Pier.* ***Far left:*** *The jetty under construction.*

Left: *The control room in the 1970s. The large mimic board has now been replaced by a modern, efficient computer system, but still controlled by an operator.*

At the Immingham Gas Terminal APT is the contracted operator of both the jetty and the Liquid Petroleum Gas (LPG) underground storage facility. There are two caverns located onshore excavated out of chalk over 200 metres below ground level. Each cavern has a capacity approaching 120,000 cubic metres (equivalent to 800 double decker buses) and both are used to store propane and butane. MV Garbetta was the first ship to use the jetty in September 1985 with the importation of 10,000 tonnes of propane. The first 'white oil' movement occurred in December 1987 when MV Esso Bombay loaded 20,000 tonnes of gas oil from Conoco's Humber Refinery.

Since the mid 1990s the tanker sizes for crude oil have been getting smaller falling to around 80,000 tonnes for shuttle tankers. Much more North Sea crude is used with a little from the Gulf/North Africa and South America.

There have been many changes since 1969, but safety has always remained the number one priority. For example even more fire fighting equipment, foam systems, pumps and personal sprays have been introduced in recent years.

APT is also systematically audited by outside expert bodies with wide industry experience to ensure the highest standards in all areas of operation are maintained.

Throughout the years the APT tank farm (the term given for the area in which tanks and associated equipment are situated) has remained basically the same although the tank products have changed. Types and specifications have developed to meet different marketing demands, such as ultra-low sulphur diesel and petrol recently.

The transportation of fuel oil for the inland market has reduced significantly as has much of the coastal trade as more product is piped direct from the refineries.

Despite the changes which have occurred in the industry each year the volume of loading and discharging has broken previous records. A total of 67 staff are currently employed divided into a small day admin/management team and five shifts providing 24 hour 365 days a year cover. In the year 2000 APT handled 26.2 million tonnes of oil on 2,772 vessels, a truly remarkable achievement.

Top left: *Two supertankers of around 200,000 tonnes in the 1970s.* ***Top right:*** *A vessel alongside Berth no. 3 at IOT.* ***Below:*** *A recent view of Immingham Oil Terminal. Note the main berths, numbering 1,2 and 3 (left to right) and the Finger Pier. The Tank Farm is in the foreground.*

Dispensing through the ages

The name of EA Broadburn above a chemist's shop is one which has now been familiar to three generations of local people. Broadburn's pharmacy at 14 St Peter's Avenue, Cleethorpes was however just the first in a small chain of similar businesses which have their origins back in January 1934.

Today the business is run by the third generation of the family, Christopher Michael Broadburn, along with his wife, Audrey Ruth Broadburn, a teacher who looks after the paperwork for the business.

It was back in 1934 that Edwin Arnold Broadburn set up his first chemist's shop. The founder had been born in 1880 and had worked in Scotland before the first world war. During the Great War Edwin joined the Royal Army Medical Corps and served in Torento in Italy.

In 1920, following his discharge from the army, Edwin married his wife Victoria and settled down to domestic life in Newsholmes in Sheffield. The couple later moved to Lincoln where their son, Edwin Walter, would be born three years later. The year following Edwin junior's birth the family moved to Cleethorpes.

The St Peter's Avenue shop was bought in 1934; at that time there was a hairdressers shop at the rear run by a Miss Haynes, now long since disappeared. The enterprise was a family affair with Edwin doing the dispensing whilst Victoria ran the shop. Chemists then were expected to make their own products using a pestle and mortar, whilst drugs such as penicillin were still unknown.

Young Edwin Walter Broadburn would grow up knowing the pharmacy business and during the second world war would find himself attending University College Nottingham studying pharmacy.

The real growth in the Broadburn pharmacy business would come with the start of the NHS in 1948 and the sudden increase in prescription dispensing which came in its wake.

For the generations who have grown up since 1948 it is difficult to imagine life before the NHS - and for many who were around in 1948, many of the critical events have now faded from memory. We are so used to having our doctors' prescription dispensed without charge, or for a relatively

Below: *A picture thought to be from the 1950s.*

modest prescription charge, it is difficult to believe that before the inauguration of the NHS many would do without medicine because they could not afford to buy it.

True, many patients were insured against ill health, through the national insurance scheme (which had its origins back in 1911) or by being members of Friendly Societies which would help cover the cost of drugs, but many, particularly women, children and the elderly did not have such cover. The NHS was intended to create a Utopian society where none should suffer for lack of income and in July 1948 the NHS came into being with, most importantly amongst its package of benefits, free medicines. In that first year 100 million free prescriptions were dispensed - only one fifth of the number dispensed today but nevertheless far more than the government had budgeted for.

Prescription charges became inevitable: famous politicians such as Bevin and Wilson resigned from the government in protest but by 1951 a charge of one shilling (5p) per form was introduced followed a few years later by a shilling per item. In subsequent years the system would change and change again and, despite a brief period without prescription charges in the 1960s, such charges have been with us ever since.

Despite the dampening effect of prescription charges demand for medicines would, however, continue to grow. By 1959 growth for Broadburn's was the order of the day when the shop next door was bought; much later, in 1982, the business premises would also incorporate outbuildings to form the large shop and storage area seen today.

Further expansion of the business would follow in due course with a former hotel, at 62 St Peter's Avenue, bought in 1982 and more two shops acquired in Scartho in the early 1990s.

The next generation of Broadburn's now looks set to continue the family tradition; whilst Christopher and Audrey's daughter Kathryn Joanne is a food technologist their other daughter Anna Elizabeth is at Bradford University studying pharmacy. Long may the Broadburn's remain local people serving local people!

Left: *Broadburn's pharmacy today.*
Top: *A family picture with Edwin standing in the centre and Edwin Walter to his left.*

More than a century of punctuality

Printing is an ancient craft thought to have been invented in China, long before its separate invention in Europe. Before printing was discovered, or reinvented, in Europe books were manuscripts - literally hand written documents - painstakingly copied out one at a time by monks working in Monasteries', 'scriptoria' producing 'illuminated', or illustrated, and costly parchments, no one of which would be exactly identical to the last.

Printing would eventually change the face of the world, producing at first lower cost books and leading in turn to an explosion in the number of literate people - and ultimately to previously unimaginable social change.

In Europe the invention of moveable type is credited to the German printer Johann Gutenburg (1400-1468) who was able to make use of the domestic metal industry to cast his type. England's first printer, William Caxton (1422-1491), learned the craft of printing in Cologne in 1471; his early books, such as that first printed in England 'Dictes or Seyengis of the Philosophres' published in 1477 in Westminster, London are now priceless.

But what has printing got to do with Grimsby, a town more associated with fishing than printing? In fact Grimsby is home to one of Britain's best known printing companies - albeit one rather less ancient than William Caxton.

It was in 1860 that Albert Gait left his home town of Brighton and bought a small book shop and printing works in Grimsby. More than 140 years later the firm which still bears the Albert Gait name is flourishing, having become one of the largest printers of timetables, manuals and technical journals in the country.

Today Albert Gait Ltd runs its famous Castle Press from its premises in the Old Castle Barracks, the prominent local landmark in Grimsby's Victoria Street.

Late in 1859, back in Queen Victoria's day, when the Albert Gait story begins, the chief office of the Postmaster of Great Grimsby was situated at 1, Market Place, a few doors away from the small news agency and book shop which the Postmaster's father, Mr William Skelton, had kept for many years. The Postmaster had been very worried as no-one had put in a bid for the business following his father's death

Above: *Company founder Albert Gait.*
Below: *Staff at work in the 1950s.*

the previous year. He certainly had no intention of carrying on the business himself, nor had his brother John Skelton who, among other things, was Danish Consul in Grimsby.

As a result of the long delay in finding a purchaser the premises had been lying shut up and derelict. Just as the brothers were despairing of ever finding a buyer for their father's business a letter arrived from Brighton expressing interest and offering, subject to certain terms, to buy the shop.

The writer, the then unknown Albert Gait, had been employed in various capacities in the printing and publishing business and most recently had been engaged in the book selling trade in the well-known house of Mr William King at No 1 North Street, Brighton. After consulting with his brother, William Skelton decided to invite Mr Gait to pay a visit to Grimsby. When Gait arrived after a long journey by train and coach the Skeltons were surprised to see such a young man. At that time Albert Gait was not more than twenty-five.

Since the value of the goodwill in the business had fallen away to almost nothing in the months since the elder Skelton's death terms were easily agreed - and the whole business was bought for £800 (of which the Gait family still have the original Bill of Sale) which left young Albert in possession of a dusty shop and a suite of empty rooms above.

Albert Gait was soon to discover that there was very little money to be made out of selling books in Grimsby. There was however some hope in developing the printing side of the business, although the equipment Albert had taken over was old and worn

Top: *Early advertising on the side of a tram, 1928.*
Above left: *Staff outside the shop circa 1900.*

out. Like many young men before, Albert soon realised that he must acquire more capital quickly in order to install the new presses and buy new type.

To supplement his income and acquire more capital Albert turned to selling patent medicine, becoming an agent for all the hundreds of remedies which perplexed and confused the public in those pre-NHS days. Not only were the famous Holloway Pills sold but such specifics and elixirs as Locock's Pulmonic Wafers, Robert's Poor Man's Friend and Smith's Scouring Drops. He also became a general advertising agent for a certain Mr R Jacques of Blackfriars in London. And if anyone had doubts about the efficacy of Albert's medicinal supplies he could always offer them his services as an agent for an insurance company.

Albert's stock of stationery was extended to cover account books, school stationery, quills, sealing wax, wafers, copybooks and slates. Even the local artist was not forgotten: London drawing boards as well as Whatman's drawing paper were available and so were Windsor and Newton's celebrated watercolours in whole and half cakes. The enterprising young man also offered new music at half price and splendid lithographs of the Corn Exchange and the Market Place. For those who couldn't afford to buy books he also instituted a circulating library in connection with Mudies. Religion and photography were not neglected either: Albert called special attention to his stock of handsome and cheap church services. Stereoscopic slides were naturally available and he also had a good selection of photographs of the royal families of England, France and Spain and all the principal celebrities of the day, whilst his large supply of microscopic photographs was acknowledged to be one of the greatest wonders of the age. Albert Gait was certainly a man of many parts.

But despite all the business diversification Albert found his heart was in printing; thanks to financial success of his other business activities he was able to acquire many new fonts of type and was soon offering to carry out letterpress printing using both black and coloured inks.

Top: *Staff pictured in the 1950s.*
Above: *Mr Harold Gait.*

It could hardly be said that Albert specialised in any one type of printing. He was ready to tackle posting bills of any magnitude, auctioneers' catalogues, cheque books, circulars, address cards and even various societies' rules, minutes and annual reports. He was also willing to repair old books and bind new ones in morroco, roan, velvet, calf or vellum. The overwhelming range of the services he was able to offer the inhabitants of Grimsby ensured his success. Gradually, as the years went by, Albert's reliance on what had become his patent medicine emporium grew less and less as the printing side of the business increased.

The function of a jobbing printer in Victorian times was essentially local, as indeed it often is for most of today's small printers. The diverse requirements imposed by a self-contained community like Grimsby ensured versatility but however they hardly encouraged fine printing and craftsmanship. The standard of Gait's work in those early days was thoroughly competent, though not in the least bit inspired. A leading designer like William Morris would have wept at the baroque type faces used and groaned aloud at the way they would be dropped piecemeal into the presses by an uninspired compositor; but the taste of the times dictated the style and who was Albert Gait to object to his customers' preferences? Neither art nor craft were Albert's guiding star; his objective was simple: he wished to make a living.

It was not until the 1890s, when Albert Gait was in his fifties, that this pupil of Samuel Smiles - the prophet of self help - extended his activities to London during the first "age of train". It happened that an ex- apprentice of Albert's, by the name of Robinson, had gone to work for the London, Brighton and South Coast Railway. Robinson, by chance, met one John Mason Cook, son of Thomas Cook, the founder of the world's largest travel organisation. John Mason Cook offered Robinson the job of editor in charge of the many tourist publications produced by Thomas Cook & Son. Robinson was, in effect, also the Print Buyer and it was in this capacity that he sought the services and assistance of

Left: *The Castle Press pictured in 1959.*
Below: *The highly skilled task of setting type, many years prior to the takeover by computers.*

his former employer and invited Albert to come down to London and see him.

The story of Albert's journey is still a legend in the Gait family. For someone who rarely travelled beyond the bounds of Grimsby the trip to London was a matter of great deliberation. Albert Gait knew that the railways charged less in those days if one travelled between stations outside the large towns; so he set out one day and walked the few miles to the first station down the line on the route to London and there booked to travel only as far as Camden Town from where he walked to Ludgate Circus in London.

The whole prospect of doing business with Thomas Cook & Son was speculative and the expense of a visit therefore had to be kept within reasonable proportions. However Albert need not have worried, nor been unduly concerned about the cost of travel. Arrangements were soon concluded with Mr Robinson and this heralded the beginning of a business relationship with Thomas Cooks that has continued for over 100 years and involved five generations of Gaits.

At first only vouchers and coupons were produced, such as price tickets for entrance to public conveniences in Brussels; but later leaflets, folders and quite large holiday programmes came off the Castle Press in the name of Thomas Cook & Son. For over 40 years the world famous Cooks Continental Timetables containing continental railway timetables together with the Overseas Timetables were produced every month at Castle Press as well as a multitude of brochures, coloured folders and vouchers for Thomas Cooks.

Other national clients soon came along too, attracted by the good quality of printing at what had become 'Castle Press' as well as its cheapness - for Albert Gait never charged fancy prices. A fair profit to him was a low one - and the more customers you had the larger the profit.

He was 73 when he died in 1907. Fortunately Albert's son, Albert Ernest (died 1947), had been brought up in the business and was able to take over. By 1960 when the firm celebrated its centenary the firm was still a family business now run by Albert's grandson Albert Harold Gait who was confidently carrying on the traditions laid down by his grandfather. Sadly, he was drowned in the Laconia disaster in 1963.

Top: *Mr Albert Gait, Mr John Price, Thomas Cook's Continental Timetable Editor and the manager of the local Thomas Cook Holiday Shop, showing the new perfect binder for their publications, 1987.*
Above: *The first Timpson 1 Up, installed at Castle Press to produce British Railways Consignment Notes.*

The large amount of 'front end capability' also enables the company to provide an excellent service to many other outside customers who only require 'origination'.

Today Albert Gait is still the printer of many of the railway and bus timetables in the country.

Printing has always been a hi-tech industry, from its earliest European origins in Gutenburg's Germany to the high speed computerised printing machines of the 21st century the industry has always utilised the latest developments. Printing led to a revolution in society: ideas could be disseminated and knowledge stored and retrieved in ever greater quantities. Science, religion, politics and commerce would never have been able to flourish without this remarkable invention, one as fundamental to human society, indeed even more fundamental, than the invention of the computer in the 20th century. Printing has become the almost invisible life blood of the modern societies, a means of transmitting and exchanging information which would become so commonplace that is now barely noticed. And yet perhaps those reading this book will spare a thought for a man, Albert Gait, who undoubtedly contributed more than he probably ever realised to the world around him.

Since the firm celebrated its centenary massive changes have taken place in the printing industry generally and not least at Albert Gait Ltd's Castle Press. Improvements in communications, both physical and electronic, have revolutionised working practices. Now comprising three distinct yet fully integrated components: printing, conventional typesetting and data manipulation, Albert Gait Ltd has moved with the times in everything but its outlook.

The printing side specialises in short to medium run mono and two colour work, mainly using B1 Miller 'perfectors' with numbering and perforation being completed on smaller presses.

A modern bindery complements the presses with facilities for automatic gathering, perfect binding and saddle stitching.

With in-house platemaking and comprehensive back up being provided by state of the art typesetting and data manipulation departments Albert Gait Ltd is well able to handle work for major clients such as The Stationery Office whilst still retaining the traditional personal touch.

Still a family business with the founders great great grandsons, Michael and Richard Gait, playing important roles, Albert Gait Ltd is now part of the large Wyndeham Press PLC Group. Michael Gait is the current Managing Director and carries on the traditions of efficiency, endeavour and enterprise handed down to him by his hard working great great grandfather.

Top left: *13 Old Market Place, Grimsby, home to Albert Gait, Booksellers for 110 years.*
Above left: *Checking film on the lightbox.*
Below: *Albert Gait, Booksellers at 49 Friargate in the Riverside Centre.*

Conjuring with chemistry

On the evening of 20 October 1951 a dinner was held at Grimsby Town Hall to celebrate the start of production at a new factory in the area. That factory now operates under the name of Novartis Grimsby Ltd. Then, however, the business being toasted by the Mayor was CIBA Laboratories, a satellite of a long established factory based at Horsham in Sussex. That Horsham factory was owned by CIBA Ltd. of Switzerland, a company founded in 1884 for research into and the manufacture of dyes before it moved into the pharmaceutical industry. In 1970 CIBA would join its assets to those of another eminent Swiss concern, J.R. Geigy, to become Ciba-Geigy Ltd., operating on an international scale and covering practically every aspect of chemistry. The well known Ciba-Geigy name, long-associated with the Grimsby factory, dates from that merger. The idea of the Grimsby plant was born in 1947 during the deepest gloom of post-war austerity in Britain when the Horsham plant proved incapable of meeting a much needed increase in production owing to an inadequate water supply and means of effluent disposal A new factory embodying those facilities was decided upon and the late J.G. Bedford, who was to become its first manager and subsequently a member of the board of directors (and who was to die tragically in 1978 following an accident whilst fox-hunting) was authorised to seek out a suitable location.

Of the many sites considered the one eventually chosen was at Pyewipe, a district of one time marshland beside the Humber estuary and then within the jurisdiction of the Lincolnshire borough of Grimsby. The name

Above: *Members of the office staff from 1957.*
Below: *The Quality Control laboratory in 1968.*

Pyewipe derives from an old name given to the plover or peewit, one of the numerous seabirds common to the area.

Amongst the considerations taken into account in making the selection was that of mutual advantage. Although an ancient port, Grimsby enjoyed little commercial standing until the advent of the railway in the late 1840's propelled it into becoming the country's major fishing centre. However it remained essentially a single industry community upon which any period slump in trade could produce disastrous results. In 1947 the local authority was anxious to attract new forms of development and was urgently promoting Pyewipe for that purpose.

In February 1948 CIBA purchased 73 acres of land from the Grimsby Corporation at £100 per acre, a contribution of £2,000 was also made towards the cost of providing railway access. Coincidence made the site particularly appropriate: part of the site included a large field called The Woads, once used for the cultivation of that oldest of dye-yielding plants.

The building contract was awarded to Richard Costain Ltd. and work began in June 1948. Progress was delayed by Government restrictions on supplies of steel, together with difficulties in obtaining construction licences. When the Duke of Edinburgh visited the site in 1949 there was still little for him to see.

It was 1950 before the obstacles were overcome and the factory rapidly began to take shape under the supervision of Messrs. Bedford, Palmer and Allen. These last two had been drawn from Horsham, being employed as chief and site engineer respectively, and gathering about them locally recruited fitters who would eventually be absorbed into the workshop department of the completed factory.

Shortages made the installation of the chemical plant a matter calling for considerable ingenuity. Steelwork salvaged from Mulberry Harbour sections used in the D-Day invasion of Normandy was pressed into service and cylindrical defence buoys were adapted for use as receivers. Some of the more sophisticated plant came from war reparations: a couple of large tile-lined tanks coming from a German V2 missile base whilst, legend

Above left: *Inspection of an RVF filter in 1968.*
Top: *Factory aerial view from 1951.*

has it that, several smaller items had seen service with the Luftwaffe.

By mid 1951 the start of production was imminent. With no nearby pool of experienced labour available the first employees had to be guided by a nucleus of trained personnel. From 1948 six locally recruited men - D. Broadley, T. Parker, T. Balderson, P. Blades, J. Elliott and G. Clarkson - had been sent to Horsham for training. With that six came staff from Horsham: general foreman J. Donelly, shift supervisors J. Cawley, M. Pyett and G. Duffield along with S. Whyatt in charge of the laboratory and L. Dunn the office administrator.

By September 1951 a small production complex had risen and was ready for use. The site consisted of three process buildings, an ice-making plant and two tank areas, one for the storage of flammable solvents and the other for chlorosulphonic acid and caustic liquor. Twin coal-burning, manually fed boilers furnished with a 120 foot high brick chimney supplied steam heating. Office, canteen, laboratory and despatch facilities were also provided for whilst engineering and maintenance services functioned from a steel frame and corrugated asbestos board building which was the original site workshop. The surroundings of the site were still unmistakably rustic: tall hedgerows and a partially demolished haystack stood close to the rear of the buildings and beyond them cultivated fields, long since built over, still stretched back towards the river Humber.

Above: *Loading finished product, bound for India.*
Right: *Demolition of the original boilerhouse chimney in the early 60s.*
Below: *View from Moody Lane in the late 1950s.*

The plant had been built to manufacture the anti-bacterial agent Sulphathiazole. The first batch was turned out on 10th November 1951 and by the end of the year a little over four tonnes had been manufactured.

Sulphonamides were to be the staple output of the factory for almost twenty years.

Disaster threatened the site on 31 January 1953 when high tides and hurricane force winds brought the sea over walls and embankments along England's East Coast. Grimsby and Pyewipe received their share of the punishment. The tide

The present name of Novartis made its appearance in 1997 following the merger of the two Swiss companies Ciba-Geigy and Sandoz in what was then the largest corporate merger ever. In 2000, Novartis achieved its strategic goal of becoming a purely healthcare company. The spin-off and subsequent merger of its Agribusiness with Zeneca Agrochemicals formed Syngenta, who now own and run one production building on the site. Novartis pharmaceutical intermediates and active ingredients are produced in three separate production buildings, whilst two others are dedicated to speciality chemical production.

poured through a breach in the Humber bank opposite the factory and finished products were stacked as high as possible in anticipation of the worst. Fortunately, due to the site being slightly higher than the surrounding land, damage was limited. Although the site was turned into a temporary island, the plant lost only one day's production.

More land was acquired over the years bringing the site to around 230 acres. Many new buildings were erected, others demolished: Building 80, for example, erected in 1977 cost more than £6 million whilst other buildings such as Building 50, an unusual 'inside out' building erected in 1959, was demolished in 1971.

A third engineering workshop was built in 1978 replacing one erected on 1959 whilst the first workshop remained in use as a store. The original boilerhouse and its brick chimney lasted until 1961 before being replaced by a modern oil fired unit which was in turn succeeded by a Combined Heat and Power Plant commissioned in 1993.
An administration block was built in 1959 and a new canteen in 1964

Further investment would follow as the years rolled on. A £240 million investment programme, for example, was announced at the beginning of 1989 making the plant Ciba's largest factory in Europe outside Switzerland. This included two new production buildings, a state of the art effluent treatment plant, a combined heat and power plant and general infrastructure improvements. The then Prime Minister John Major conducted the official opening of the new facilities in 1993. Around half of the 230 acre site is currently developed.

The Novartis staff support many local groups such as the Lincolnshire Wildlife Trust and the Royal Society for the Protection of Birds. Sponsorship is also given to groups such as the Caxton Theatre where employees are actively involved both as performers and behind the scenes!

As a holder of three Queen's Awards for Export Achievement, Novartis is not just one of the town's major employers but its existence stands as a testament to the foresight of both the company and the local authority in making use of the Pyewipe site for industrial development more than fifty years ago.

Above: *The Board and 25 Year Club in 1984.*
Below: *Novartis as seen in the early 1990s.*

A small corner of history

The corner shop is a British institution. Often it is the hub of community life; some of our earliest memories are of visiting the local shop to spend our Saturday pennies and in later years of being despatched with a half crown wrapped in a shopping list once our mothers deemed us old enough to go there on our own.

Not even Grimsby's oldest resident however will now recall the opening of the Ripon Street Post Office and Costcutter corner shop.

Today the shop offers a full range of supermarket products and food items, lottery tickets, Post Office services, a newsagency and also an off licence. The shop was founded in the early part of the last century by JR Plaskett and run by his family for many years until it was purchased from a Mr Smedley by its present owners, the Bradley family.

Since then three generations have been involved in running the store. Margaret and Cedric Bradley who bought the shop from the Smedleys were in turn succeeded by their son Robert and his wife Marilyn Bradley and now they have been joined in partnership by their son, Scott.

Below: *The premises as they were in the early 1900s.*

Back in 1954 it was Cedric who ran the Post Office whilst Margaret ran the shop. Previously Cedric had been a plumber in Grimsby whilst Margaret had earned her living as a local hairdresser. Cedric in fact originally hailed from Leeds whilst Margaret was from the neighbouring city of Bradford though they met in Grimsby and liked the place enough to decide to stay. The small corner shop with living accommodation above on Ripon Street may not have been anything marvellous at the time but the Bradleys clearly saw its potential for growth.

In the late 1950s the first opportunity to expand the shop arrived. The next door premises became vacant and were bought: the Post Office part of the business was moved in there. The 1960s would see further development with the family knocking through into the ground floor living accommodation and moving themselves upstairs to provide more shop space.

When 'buying groups' first started in the 1960s the Bradleys joined in and over the years the shop has traded under the names of Centra, Spar, VG and, since 1987, Costcutter. Margaret was very much her own woman with a strong will and didn't always care to be told what to do by others however: when Green Shield Stamps came out in the 1960s she wanted to have the stamps. Spar told her she could not so she finished with Spar and went with the VG buying group instead.

Further business expansion followed in 1965 when another shop was bought in Springbank. The Springbank shop was however subsequently sold in 1971 in order to concentrate on developing Ripon Street.

Cedric Bradley died in 1976 and his son Robert started in the business the following year. Robert and his mother were partners until she died in 1987. Robert's wife Marilyn worked in the shop with Robert and Margaret until Margaret retired at which time Marilyn took charge of the Post Office. Following Margaret Bradley's death the rear yard was built over expanding the shop and storage areas. And in 1990 the next house along was bought and a major refurbishment embarked upon moving the Post Office into the new part and totally refitting the premises to today's high standard. The shop was further upgraded during the 1990s with new units and new tills.

The year 1992 saw Robert and Marilyn's son Scott come into the business full time though typically of a family concern both he and his sister Claire had worked in the business from being teenagers.

The fact that one corner shop can have been owned and run by so few families in the hundred years or so of its history is almost unique. Three generations of the Bradley family have now served their customers at their Ripon Street store and three generations of customers have benefited from a friendly personal service from people who know even their names - so different from the impersonal supermarket experience we have had to come to terms with. Long may the Bradleys continue to run their store - and who knows, with luck, maybe a fourth generation will emerge to continue running this thoroughly modern, yet wholly traditional corner shop, for another hundred years.

***Above:** Margaret and Cedric Bradley.*
***Right:** Robert, Marilyn and Scott outside the shop.*

From webbed feet to websites

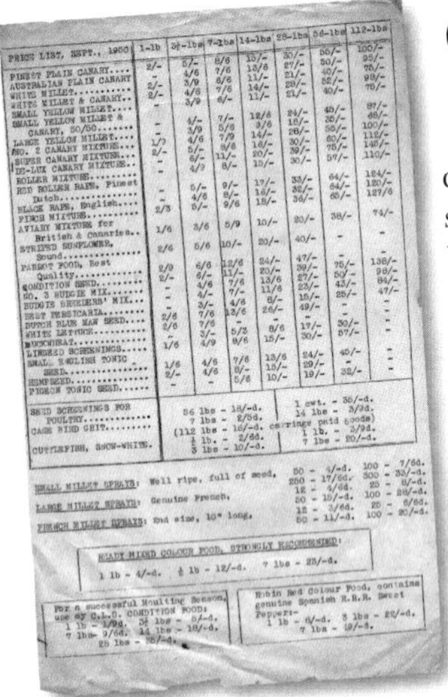

PRICE LIST, SEPT., 1950 | 1-lb | 3½-lbs | 7-lbs | 14-lbs | 28-lbs | 56-lbs | 112-lbs

FINEST PLAIN CANARY....
AUSTRALIAN PLAIN CANARY
WHITE MILLET..........
WHITE MILLET & CANARY..
SMALL YELLOW MILLET....
SMALL YELLOW MILLET & CANARY, 50/50.......
LARGE YELLOW MILLET....
NO. 2 CANARY MIXTURE...
SUPER CANARY MIXTURE...
DE-LUX CANARY MIXTURE..
ROLLER MIXTURE.........
RED ROLLER RAPE, Finest Dutch..............
BLACK RAPE, English....
FINCH MIXTURE..........
AVIARY MIXTURE for British & Canaries..
STRIPED SUNFLOWER, Sound..............
PARROT FOOD, Best Quality.............
CONDITION SEED.........
NO. 3 BUDGIE MIX.......
BUDGIE BREEDERS' MIX...
BEST PERSICARIA........
DUTCH BLUE MAW SEED....
WHITE LETTUCE..........
BUCKWHEAT..............
LINSEED SCREENINGS.....
SMALL ENGLISH TONIC SEED...............
HEMPSEED...............
PIGEON TONIC SEED......

SEED SCREENINGS FOR POULTRY.............
CAGE BIRD GRIT.........
CUTTLEFISH, SNOW-WHITE.

SMALL MILLET SPRAYS: Well ripe, full of seed,
LARGE MILLET SPRAYS: Genuine French.
FRENCH MILLET SPRAYS: 2nd size, 10" long.

READY MIXED COLOUR FOOD, STRONGLY RECOMMENDED:
1 lb - 4/-d. ½ lb - 12/-d. 7 lbs - 25/-d.

For a successful Moulting Season, use my C.L.O. CONDITION FOOD:

Robin Red Colour Food, contains genuine Spanish R.R.R. Sweet Pepper:-

'Feed the birds, tuppence a bag...' we can all recall the chorus to the well loved song which featured in Walt Disney's Mary Poppins; at some time or another we have all kept cage birds or fed wild ones, but where does birdseed come from? For more than fifty years now the answer to that particular question has more often than not been Cleethorpes.

John E Haith Ltd is now a nationally, and indeed internationally, famed birdseed supplier. After more than half a century in business Haiths have unrivalled experience supplying birdfoods by mail order direct to customers' doors. The business was founded in the 1930s by John 'Ted' Haith who later developed the mail order side of the business from his small shop in Park Street in Cleethorpes.

Before opening up in Park Street however 'Ted' Haith had earlier worked as Sutcliffe's private zoo in Grimsby where he gained experience in caring for animals before opening his first pet shop in Grimsby Road, Cleethorpes in the late thirties. That first shop would remain part of the business until the 1960s. Before any such expansion could be thought of however along came the war. During the second world war Ted Haith joined the local volunteers in the fire service working with them at night whilst keeping his shop during the day.

Following the end of the second world war, in 1947, a new pet shop in Park Street was opened. An old Methodist chapel was bought which was converted into a shop and warehouse to which offices were to be added in the 1950s. From the outset Ted Haith quickly began to specialise in birdseed and soon developed a mail order business.

In the 1940s and 50s there were many companies

Left: *A price list of the company's products from 1950.* ***Below:*** *Grimsby Cage Bird Society in 1928.* ***Bottom:*** *The premises in the 1940s.*

selling birdseed by mail order and competition was fierce. Haiths however managed to cause a storm at the 1950 Trade Show when the company had a stand containing 40,000 envelopes and revealed that each one was an order received the previous month.

Perhaps it was the sheer range of stock kept by the firm which contributed to its triumph. Or perhaps it was equally down to Ted Haith's business skill and specialist knowledge. Whatever the winning combination a look through the catalogues serves to astonish and delight. Even the inexpert can't fail to appreciate the magic contained in such exotic sounding names as Japanese Millet, Lovebird Mixture or Moroccan Canary seed.

And that's not all. What can the novice make of 'Naked Oats', and 'Mixed Pulses', 'Squirrel Mix' and 'A1 fancy Pigeon Mixture'

By the 1960s the business was so large that three houses were bought to accommodate expansion of the firm's warehouses.

Since its beginnings three generations of the Haith family have been involved in the birdseed business. In the year 2000 Ted's grandson David bought the full shareholding of the family's business to continue the Haith tradition of supplying high quality super-clean birdseeds.

After more than fifty years the business is still mainly selling birdseed with tens of thousands of customers nation-wide divided almost equally between on the one hand cage and aviary bird owners and, on the other, RSPB members. And not only in Britain, the firm also has a thriving mail order business with thousands of customers throughout Europe. Today Haiths remains one of the very few firms still selling birdseed by mail order and everyone in the bird world knows of the company and its outstanding reputation built up over more than half a century.

Whether one keeps parrots or pigeons, budgies or bantams, canaries or cockatiels, of one thing customers can be sure: Haiths of Cleethorpes will always have exactly the right kind of birdfood in stock.

Today the company website is generating a tremendous amount of interest and the company is about to launch ordering facilities by e-mail. A new computerised system was installed in 2000. The use of computers and all its associated technology may be a long way from what was in John 'Ted' Haith's mind when he founded his new enterprise back in the 1940s but his commitment to quality products and a personal informed and expert service to clients continues to this day.

Above left: *The staff in the 1950s.*
Top: *Office staff in the 1950s.*

Children at a Labour Party on May Day in 1923.

NELC Grimsby Local Studies Library

Acknowledgments

The publishers would like to thank Garry Crossland, MA for his help in the course of research and proof-reading; Associated British Ports and North East Lincolnshire Council Libraries, Grimsby Local Studies Library.

Thanks are also due to Margaret Wakefield who penned the editorial text and Steve Ainsworth for his copywriting skills